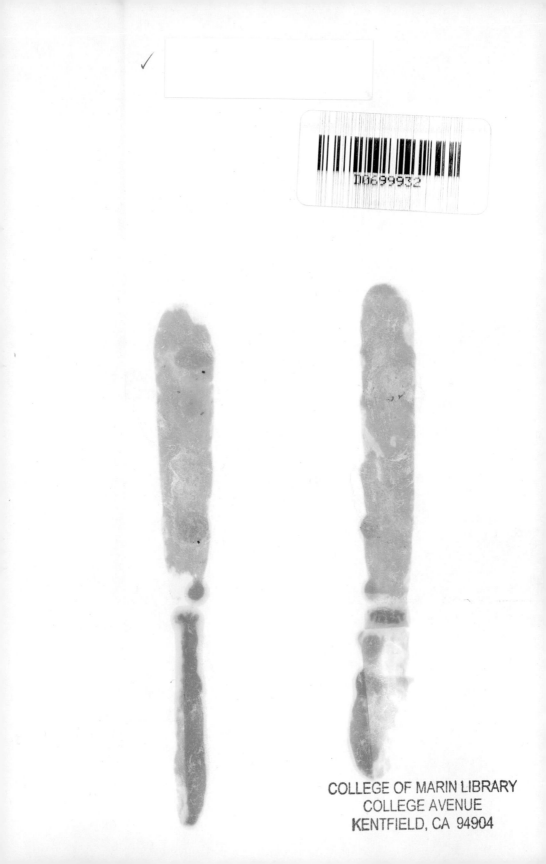

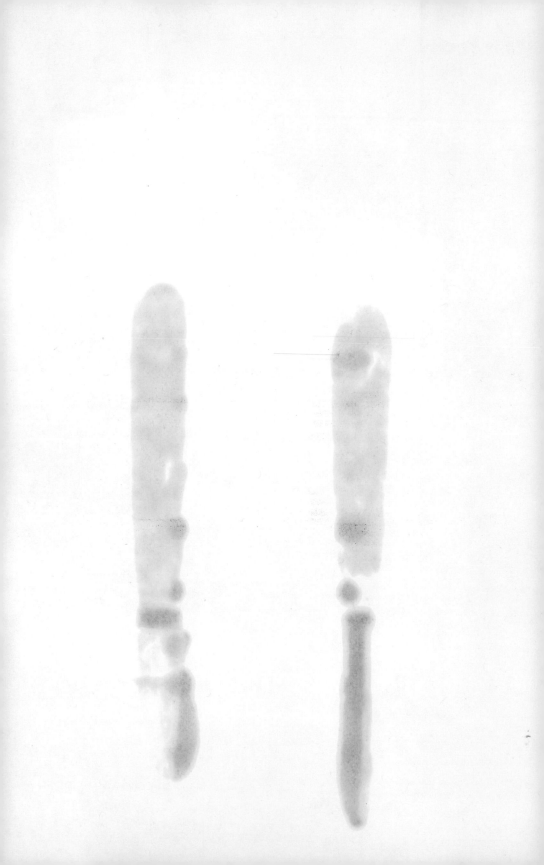

North of Reconstruction
Ohio Politics, 1865–1870

North of Reconstruction Ohio Politics, 1865–1870

by

Felice A. Bonadio

1970

NEW YORK: New York University Press

For Betty

Author's Preface and Acknowledgments

Experience suggests that in the ordinary course general histories of the reconstruction era have focused attention upon major events at what may be called, for convenience, the national level of politics. Monographs on reconstruction, save for those concerned primarily with the South, have also concentrated on national politics in their treatment of the issues that occupied the attention of political leaders in this period of American history. Studies of particular states, areas, or regions of the North are often out of date or else depend for their conclusions upon material that is sometimes inadequate or incomplete.

My purpose is to examine the politics of a single Northern state, Ohio, in the years that followed the Civil War.[1] Ohio was selected for a variety of reasons. It was a key political state in the North—a fact attested to by the deliberate and diligent attention which the two major parties paid to it in the post-Civil War period. Also, a vigorous competition developed between the two major parties in Ohio, which makes the politics of the state a more valuable source of commentary than would have been the case for a state the political life of which was dominated by a single party. Finally, Ohio's political leaders played a significant part—more than in most Northern states —in determining the course of American politics in the post-Civil War period—some, indeed, with much success.

The great political contest which raged in the North in the years that followed the Civil War was dominated by the twin issues of Southern reconstruction and Negro rights. By design, therefore, no attempt is made in this book to deal with Ohio politics in a detailed and comprehensive manner. Rather, certain aspects of the politics of that state are discussed in the context of the public debate over these two issues. My purpose has been to shed further light on the relationship between them and the course of politics in a single Northern state.

The major theme of the book is that Ohio's political leaders were less concerned with a sincere discussion of the two issues of Southern reconstruction and Negro rights than historians have commonly assumed. Unconsciously, perhaps, historians, dominated by their studies of great national questions, have superimposed certain ideologies upon ordinary political developments in the post-Civil War period, sometimes in a misleading way.

As this study suggests, ideology had little place in the political struggles of these years, at least in Ohio. And it may be that Ohio's example can serve as a pointer to indicate other fruitful areas for study in this general period of our history.[2]

I would like to express my appreciation for the help and encouragement given to me by Professors Howard R. Lamar and C. Vann Woodward, who concerned themselves with this work from its earliest stages. I owe a very great debt to Professor Robin Winks, whose help, encouragement, and friendship over many years have been immensely valuable to me. I am also indebted to Professors Otey Scruggs and John F. H. New, who read this book in typescript.

I must express my warm thanks to Professors David M.

Potter and Harold Hyman, who read all or part of this study and furnished me with many valuable suggestions. I am most grateful to Professor Alfred Gollin, in particular, who was extremely generous in his exacting criticism and wise counsel.

I should like also to record my debt to many librarians in various parts of the country. They are: David C. Mearns of the Library of Congress, Kenneth Duckett of the Ohio State Library, Watt Marchmann of the Rutherford B. Hayes Library, and Mrs. Alice P. Hook of the Historical and Philosophical Society of Cincinnati. The staffs of the libraries at Oberlin College, Western Reserve University, and the University of California, Santa Barbara were also very helpful.

Mrs. Alice Kladnik typed the manuscript with care and patience and I want to express my thanks to her. Sam and Sue Adams kindly proofread the entire typescript, and I should like to record my gratitude to them.

The person to whom I owe the greatest debt of gratitude is my wife, who deserves much better than the dedication of this book.

NOTES

1. For a detailed discussion of Republican politics in Ohio in the prewar period see David H. Bradford, "The Background and Formation of the Republican Party in Ohio, 1844–1861" (unpublished Ph.D. dissertation, Department of History, University of Chicago, 1947).

2. The two standard accounts of Ohio politics in the post-Civil War period are George H. Porter, *Ohio Politics During the Civil War* (New York, 1911); Eugene H. Roseboom, *The Civil War Era, 1850–1873* (Columbus, 1944). A recent book that contains much useful information on Republican politics in Ohio is George H. Mayer, *The Republican Party, 1854–1964* (New York, 1964), pp. 108–15.

Contents

North of Reconstruction
Ohio Politics, 1865–1870

The Imaginary Party

CHAPTER ONE

I

The elections of October, 1865, marked a turning point in the history of the Republican party in Ohio. Although Jacob D. Cox, the Republican candidate for governor, won the election, the party leaders had every reason to feel disappointed and anxious. Cox's majority was the smallest in the history of the party, 29,000 votes, whereas in 1861 and 1865, the Republican majority had been 55,000 and 100,000 respectively.[1] Further, the autumn elections of 1867 made the declining popularity of the Republicans even plainer, for the Democrats won control of the state legislature, and their candidate for governor lost his own contest by a mere 3000 votes. These Democratic gains seemed so menacing to Republican politicians that they openly discussed their fears about the future of their party in the state of Ohio. "The Republican party is rapidly going to pieces," complained a correspondent; "it has ever been composed of discordant elements." [2]

1

There were valid reasons for the waning strength of the Republican party in Ohio in the years immediately following the Civil War. Despite the patriotic identification of Republicanism with the North's victory over the South, the party was far less strong in 1865 than it had been before the war began. This was chiefly due to the party factionalism that had existed before the war began and which became even more pronounced after the war ended.[3] That is, in 1855 Republican ex-Whigs and Democrats had joined forces with the antislavery Democrats to found the Republican party. At first, there were some differences between these two groups, but they seemed minor. As the new party became more powerful, however, and especially after it took control of the state, the minor differences of earlier days were magnified. The split became apparent, for example, at the Republican National Convention of 1860, at which Salmon P. Chase, an ex-Democrat, was being considered for the presidential nomination.[4] Prior to the convention, Chase's chances for the nomination had been good, among other reasons, because his party in Ohio had pledged him its support. However, once the convention began, this pledge was broken by the ex-Whigs in the Ohio Republican delegation. Chase failed to win the support of his home state and lost the nomination. The party displayed the same discord again in 1864. On this occasion the Republican followers of the ex-Whig Benjamin F. Wade went so far as to break party ranks in order to defeat Chase in his attempt.[5] (Four years later Chase was denied the nomination once more, even before the Republican convention in Chicago had a chance to convene.)

Differences between Republican ex-Whigs and Democrats reached down to almost every congressional district and county in the state. Personal disagreements and the memories of old battles were involved as well as disagreements over current political issues. More seriously, however, disputes over political patronage made the disagreements even more intense as the factions snatched at the spoils of office while they tried to block the maneuvers of their opponents. Thus, former Democrats believed that the ex-Whigs were mere opportunists who had only moved into the party for reasons of expediency and narrow advantage.[6] There was evidence for this view. Until 1852, when their party dissolved, the Whigs had quarreled among themselves over the issue of Negro slavery. Their sudden enthusiasm for a new party dedicated to the containment of the institution of slavery seemed to many Democrats like a devious attempt to restore the Whig party to life and to power. Ex-Democrats like William C. Howells, the fiery editor of the Ashtabula *Sentinel,* warned against trusting "eleventh hour workers" who were less dedicated to reform than to political office.[7]

There also was a division between the Republicans and the War Democrats, who had entered the Republican party following a serious controversy. The outbreak of the Civil War split the Democratic party in Ohio into three hostile factions. One group, known as the "State Sovereignty Democrats," refused to support the Northern war effort. A second group of Democrats, who called themselves "Moderates," supported the war but advocated an early peace settlement with the South. A third group of Democrats, the "War Democrats," believed that the war had to be fought until the North achieved victory over the South.[8]

In 1861 the Republicans had proposed that the war be fought on a bipartisan basis and had changed the name of their party from "Republican" to "Union" to make it easier for Democrats to join them in a political alliance, the primary object of which was a more effective prosecution of the war.[9] This informal alliance worked successfully for a short period of time. However, partisanship soon intervened when, in 1862, a popular revulsion against the war swept the North, and the Democrats changed their attitude. All the resources of their party were then brought to bear on rallying an opposition to the war. The Democratic party became the party of peace.[10] Democrats advocated an immediate cease-fire on terms that would impose no punishment on the South for its secession from the Union. In this way they sought to impress upon the public that the responsibility for continued fighting rested upon the Republicans.

Not all Democrats agreed with this position. A group

calling themselves "War Democrats" instantly assailed this new policy, arguing that peace without victory was unacceptable to those who believed that the principle of secession threatened America's progress as an independent nation. They hastened to join the Republican party.[11]

The Republican leaders in Ohio welcomed the War Democrats for two reasons, to strengthen their own party and to continue the semblance of a bi-partisan character to the war effort. But a dissenting voice was raised by local Republicans, who claimed that the share of political offices received by the War Democrats outweighed their actual worth to the party. "I am tired of having the state governed by that [War Democratic] element of the Union forces," one district worker complained. "It furnishes about a tenth of the votes and has gotten about nine tenths of the offices." [12] This argument, however, was true neither during the war nor after it. But the fact that War Democrats gained any offices at all was enough to plant jealousy in the hearts of local Republican politicians in many parts of the state.

Jealousy of this kind made itself felt during the war period on a number of occasions. In 1861 David Tod, a War Democrat, was selected by the Republican State Convention as the party's candidate for governor. Although he succeeded in the election of 1861, Tod was unable to secure renomination for the post two years later because of the opposition of a number of Republican groups.[13] The same fate overtook John Brough, another War Democrat, who won the governorship in 1863. Two years later, when the time came for Brough's renomination, so much hostility had arisen against his cause within the ranks of his own party that his closest friends urged him to abandon his candidacy rather than risk a major disruption of their party.[14] Three days before the Republican convention of 1865 began, Brough addressed a public letter to the "people" of Ohio. In it, he wrote frankly about the "conflicts" that would arise if he allowed his name to be brought before them. He concluded by withdrawing his name from the convention.[15] In each of these cases no major issue of policy was involved. Both Tod and Brough were victims of petty party jealousies that were essentially unimportant save for the results they produced.

It is thus clear that in the period from 1861 to 1865 the Republican party in Ohio was torn by serious internal dissensions. In 1857 Republican leaders had hoped, with reason, for a majority that would enable them to control state politics indefinitely. By 1865, it had become obvious to all that party factionalism had prevented them from realizing their ambition. The rivalry between the ex-Whigs and the ex-Democrats had opened an ominous crack in the structure of the party. The union with the War Democrats, far from adding strength, had promoted additional strains which gave rise to vicious political battles, and, in several districts, paralyzed the party completely. Only the war unified the party to survive these crises; it made Republican majorities appear more impressive than they actually were.

II

Apart from the bitterness involved, the most damaging result of Republican factionalism was the creation of third parties in Ohio by dissatisfied Democrats and dissident Republicans who, for a variety of reasons, had abandoned all hope of living within their own party. During the war years, third party movements were confined to a few congressional districts. However, peace brought an intensification of intraparty rivalries, and these movements spread throughout the state, causing turmoil worse than anything that had occurred in the entire history of the party. "The Republican party," one writer declared, "is in a fit condition of self-murder." [16]

The most volatile of these third party movements began during the war in Ohio's tenth congressional district, which included Toledo. This district was represented in Congress by James Ashley, an ex-Democrat, who had been elected in 1860.[17] At the Republican convention of 1862 Ashley was nominated for a second term. But he was nominated only after a bitter struggle with a group of ex-Whigs from Toledo. They opposed his return to Congress because they felt he was indifferent to the commercial and business requirements of Toledo, the chief city in his congressional district. On September 27, 1866, The *Toledo Daily Blade* reported of certain Republicans that they "find fault with Mr. Ashley because Toledo secured a smaller appropriation than some other cities on the lakes." Ashley found it necessary to call upon the assistance of Republican leaders outside the state in order to refute the charge.[18]

The ex-Whigs formed the Independent party to oppose Ashley and selected Morrison B. Waite as the candidate for Congress.[19] They were anxious to secure harbor improvements for the city, a more extensive system of railway communication, and all those developments that might enable Toledo to compete more efficiently with cities like Cleveland and Cincinnati. Moreover, it had been learned in 1862 that Ashley had abused his position as Chairman of the Committee on Territories in Congress by releasing confidential information to certain friends in Colorado, thus enabling them to purchase land that was to be used by the federal government in its railway program in the Far West. This became known when letters written to Frank Case, whom Ashley had supported for the position as Surveyor General of Colorado in 1861, were published in the *Cleveland Plain Dealer* on January 11, 1867. They were subsequently referred to by Ashley's enemies in the tenth district as the "Dear Case" letters. In one of these letters, dated March 18, 1861, and marked "strictly confidential," Ashley wrote:

> Everything hangs on a hair. . . . I have promised all the subordinate places under you. . . . I ask for three of the places myself and give the rest to other members who are helping me. . . . I want to have an interest with you, if I get the place in the city and town lot speculations. The Pacific Railroad will go through this territory, and it will be fortunate to us if I can get it. . . . I will probably be Chairman of Committee on Territories, if I can carry out the programme to elect Grow Speaker, and your brother Charles Case of Indiana Clerk, and then I

will know all the proposed expenditures in the Territories, and post you in advance.

The publication of Ashley's letters proved to be a serious embarrassment to the Republican party and a boon of some political consequence to the Democrats.

The clash between Ashley and the Independents produced
results of genuine consequence. In the fall elections of 1862
Ashley managed to carry his district only by a plurality of
39 percent of the total vote. Moreover, Morrison Waite, his
Independent rival, actually won a plurality of 1216 votes over
Ashley in the city of Toledo, which Ashley had carried with
ease two years earlier. The Republican factions themselves had
succeeded in turning a safe district into a doubtful one because
of this mutual jealousy and rivalry.

This election has attracted the attention of historians for
several reasons. For one, they have studied the election to try
to make clear the reasons for the electoral losses of the Republicans on the national level. (In the congressional elections of
1862, the Republican party lost five states in the North that
it had won in the presidential contest two years earlier.) Some
historians have argued that Ashley and other Republicans lost
votes because President Lincoln's administration had failed to
gain any significant military victories by 1862. Moreover, they
claim that Republican candidates also did badly as a result of
Lincoln's promulgation of the Emancipation Proclamation.[20]
However, we must notice that Ashley's political fate cannot be
explained adequately on these terms alone. In 1864 Lincoln,
having won substantial military victories, was reelected with
a large majority, as were many other Republican candidates.[21]
However, James Ashley did not share their good fortune in the
election of 1864. In his district he was still plagued by the
alliance between the Independents and the Democrats. Although he managed to win the election, it was by a bare
margin of less than 900 votes. It seems clear that local rather
than national issues were the determining factors in his case.

The serious nature of the revolt of the ex-Whigs forced

Ashley to react boldly. He decided to form his own party in Ohio. Ashley believed that the nucleus of this "new party" would be composed of the War Democrats, for it seemed clear to him that his appearance before the electors as a Republican candidate could not ensure his return to office. On August 5, 1864, he wrote to Salmon P. Chase: "I am pledged by the action of the convention which nominated me to vote for Mr. Lincoln, but I am free to act with loyal Democrats in advising the permanent organization of the War Democrats into a great National Party, which properly managed could take possession of the Great Government in 1868—even if they fail now."

Ashley turned to Washington MacLean, the Democratic editor of the *Cincinnati Daily Enquirer,* in order to propose an arrangement or an alliance. This scheme was reported to President Andrew Johnson on July 4, 1865, by R. P. L. Baber, a local politician of some influence in Columbus. Baber wrote to President Johnson: "The Chase-Ashley party have already made propositions to unite with the Copperhead Opposition— a happy riddance for they opposed you at the Baltimore Convention."

MacLean, at this time, was also encountering difficulties in the conduct of his political affairs. During the war he had been a leader of the peace movement in the state and in this way he had exposed his fellow Democrats to the charge of treason. In consequence, the Ohio Democrats were trying to force him out of the party in order to protect its image in the public mind.[22] Ashley calculated that, in these circumstances, MacLean might welcome an arrangement of some kind that would enable him to continue to play some part in the political life of the state. Ashley, in other words, was quite ready to sacrifice his principles in an attempt to secure the political survival of both.

Ashley's plan, however, failed to bear fruit. In MacLean's opinion, the political situation was far too unsettled for him to commit himself to Ashley or to anyone else in a third party movement. "He [MacLean] is quite at sea as to what course to pursue"—thus wrote Edward Carson, a Cincinnati postmaster and politician of some skill in intrigue, and the chief negotiator employed during these delicate transactions, to Chase on January 23, 1865. MacLean sent a polite but evasive reply and Ashley abandoned all hope of the arrangement. As a result of his failure to secure an alliance with MacLean, Ashley found it necessary to remain within the Republican party, and he continued to be criticized for those lapses which had aroused opposition to him in the first place.[23]

James Ashley's political life was saved when President Andrew Johnson broke with the mass of his party over the issue of reconstruction. The heat of the dispute momentarily fused Republican sentiments, for the closing of Republican ranks against Johnson inclined the party to accept its incumbent leadership. Although Ashley's enemies continued to plan his political defeat and ruin in 1866, he was renominated to Congress at the Republican convention in Toledo by acclamation.[24] However, by 1868, the year of Grant's election, the Republican party enjoyed a harmony and a unity of a kind that had escaped it for a very long time. (See Chapter Five.) In these circumstances it was at last possible for the Independents to bring their fierce campaign against Ashley to its logical conclusion. No one understood this fact any better than Ashley himself. After his defeat Ashley addressed a letter to his constituents in the tenth district, published in the *Toledo Daily Blade* on November 17, 1868. In it, he wrote: "I was entitled to the support of every true Republican. Instead of receiving such support I was defeated by falsehood, treachery and fraud. . . . No man can be regarded as a faithful party man who either openly or secretly confederates with the enemy." Even though Grant won the election the opposition to Ashley was so severe that he was unable to share in the general success of his party. "Facts are facts," the *Toledo Blade* commented on October 10, 1868. "Mr. Ashley had more opposition in the Republican party than any other man in this district."

III

We should notice that the Independent campaign which finally toppled Ashley was not any more acrimonious and bitter than many other struggles that had taken place elsewhere in Ohio. For example, during the war the third congressional district, containing Dayton, had been a strong base of Republican support. In the fall of 1865 Daniel Haynes, the most popular Republican in the district and Judge of the Superior Court, stood for re-election. He wanted the nomination and had strong claims for it, but he was denied it because the ex-Democrats in his party proposed a candidate of their own for the office. They were determined to punish him for running as an Independent in 1861, and for soliciting the aid of the Democratic party at that time. With consummate skill, these ex-Democrats managed to replace Haynes with John Lowe, an ex-Union officer, at the Republican convention.[25]

This contest entered its second phase when Haynes' supporters formed an Independent party in order to strike back at the Republicans.[26] These Independents succeeded in reaching an understanding with the Democrats. Their negotiations resulted in an alliance of mutual support. "The smartest sort of Republicans," wrote the *Dayton Journal* on September 21, 1865, "seem willing to play into the hands of a party whose principles they despise." Again, in an attack upon Haynes and his supporters, the *Dayton Journal* on October 5, 1865, declared: "As their case is a bad one, they are forced to extraordinary expedients. They are pitted against the people of the Union party. They know that if they succeed, it will not be by Union votes, but by the votes of Copperheads." The Democrats in the third district were overjoyed by the arrangement with Haynes, and openly approved of it. "The Democracy of Dayton," they stated in a circular reprinted in the *Dayton Journal* on October 10, 1865, "are a unit upon this question. We will all vote for Judge Haynes."

In the October elections Haynes was victorious. The ramifications of the Independent schism went far beyond the contest for the judgeship. With one exception, the entire Republican ticket in the district was defeated.[27] On October 13, 1865, the *Journal,* the chief organ of the party in the district deplored the "family fuss" which had "demoralized" the party and kept Republican voters at home. The more optimistic among the Republicans saw this outcome as merely a temporary setback, a convenient explanation in that it minimized the party's difficulties. Only in the fall of 1866 did these Republicans come to understand the full implication of the Independent movement.

One year later, in the October elections of 1866, Republicans in the third district renominated Congressman Robert Schenck. The Democrats made no nomination. This tactic had, by the fall of 1866, become a typically Democratic course in Montgomery County. In the municipal elections in the spring of that year the Democrats made no nomination for the position of mayor of Dayton. Instead, they voted to support John Kenney, who ran as an Independent against the candidate of the Republican party. (See the *Dayton Journal,* March 6, 1866.) In that election, Kenney was victorious. The *Dayton Journal* on April 4, 1866, commented: "The election of Mr. Kenney was a *personal* victory. . . . There was not an element of party success in it. Had the plain issue of Union man or Copperhead been acted upon by the people he would have been beaten." For their part, however, the Democrats thought otherwise. On April 7, they were quoted by the *Dayton Journal* stating that the results of the elections were "a great Democratic victory." Likewise, the Democrats voted to support Durbin Ward for Congress, a Republican who ran on an Independent ticket. However, this was not done without protest from some Democrats in the third district; Ward's name was placed in nomination before a convention of Independent Republicans and Democrats in Dayton. Richard Cunningham, a Democrat from Preble County, was quoted in the *Dayton Journal* on August 29, 1866, denouncing Ward as "a mongrel who is unfit for Democrats to vote for." (Republicans were also quoted, in the *Dayton Journal* of August 31 and September 1, 1866, making attacks upon Ward.)

Schenck was reelected to Congress by a majority of 1067 votes out of a total of 28,987 votes cast. A year earlier, Republicans had dismissed the Independent party as a fly-by-night affair. But with this reappearance, it loomed as a sinister threat. Now reflective Republicans in the district could foresee a time when their man could easily be defeated. This fear was borne out two years later when Schenck was reelected to Congress by the slim margin of 475 votes. By 1870 Schenck's Republican opposition in his district finally achieved their purpose. In the congressional elections of that year he lost his seat in Congress to Lewis Campbell, who ran as an Independent Republican.

In addition to causing trouble in Schenck's district, the Independent movement also produced serious consequences in the second congressional district, which included Cincinnati. The city of Cincinnati, in Hamilton County, was composed of two congressional districts—the first and the second. Since 1863 the second district had been represented in Congress by Rutherford B. Hayes. However, in 1867 Hayes resigned his congressional seat to become the Republican candidate for governor in the state elections of that year. Hayes's resignation resulted in a fight between Republicans in the district to become congressman in his place.

Toward the end of 1865 Murat Halstead, editor of the *Cincinnati Daily Commercial,* led a movement to form a third party in the district by calling for an alliance between the "conservative" men of both parties. "That new parties will arise," the *Commercial* declared, "who can question? They are demanded, and the demand in politics is always supplied." [28] This alliance, Halsted claimed, would begin a "Conservative" or "People's" party which, if well managed, would be free of unresolved rivalries and would become the basis for a new statewide organization. The reaction of Republicans to Halstead's plan for a new statewide party was generally hostile.[29]

The new party did not make its appearance in the district until the summer of 1867, and when it did appear it was not the organization that Halstead had hoped to create. At that time, a coalition of Republican ex-Whigs, War Democrats, and trade unionists formed the Workingman's party. The party nominated Samuel Carey to oppose Richard Smith, editor of the *Cincinnati Daily Gazette,* for a seat in the House of Representatives. On September 10, 1867, Smith declared in the *Gazette,* "At length a portion of the members of the Trades Union, having determined to turn their society into a political party, have nominated Mr. Carey as their candidate for Representative, and he has accepted." [30] We should notice that Carey, a War Democrat, had lost the nomination to Smith at the Republican convention a month earlier.[31] The chief sop to the trade union members for this new alliance was a vague program for limiting the hours of labor, and a still vaguer one for improving the status of the workingman. In fact, this concern for the urban worker was a mere pretext. The main purpose of the new party was to divide the vote of the Republicans in the district, and thus make certain the defeat of Smith. An editorial in the *Cincinnati Daily Gazette,* September 11, 1867, summed up the attitude of most Republicans in the second district toward Carey's nomination. "This movement . . . could have no other rational purpose than to throw off his honorable obligations to abide by the result of the Convention before which he had been a candidate. . . . Mr. Carey seems to have no political or moral perceptions. He is simply a 'disappointed office seeker' who sought the nomination from any faction that would divide the Republican vote."

The campaign that followed was sensational for the heights, or depths, of denunciation reached by candidates Carey and Smith. While insults were flying, MacLean added the influence of the *Enquirer* to Carey's cause, thus creating even more confusion for the Republicans. Furthermore, in the 1867 election the Democrats in the second district decided not to nominate one of their own number to fill the vacant congressional seat. Instead, they voted to support Carey for that position. The Republicans were quoted by the *Cincinnati Daily Gazette* on September 11, 1867: "Mr. Carey presents himself before the people of this District as the candidate of the coalition promised to him by the *Enquirer* between the Democrats

and such Republicans as he can disaffect. . . . He is in fact
the Democratic candidate, with the promise of carrying over
a portion of the Republicans to that party." [32]

Also, a few days before the election, Charles Reemelin, a
prominent Republican leader in Cincinnati, revealed the "arrangement" between Carey and the Democrats in a speech
quoted in the *Cincinnati Daily Gazette* of September 30, 1867.
"The secret treaty," Reemelin declared, "is that the Democratic vote of the Second Congressional District shall be cast
for Carey, in consideration of his friends supporting the general Democratic ticket."

As had the election in Dayton in the previous year, this
election destroyed what had been a Republican stronghold in
the state. Smith was defeated, and he dragged the bulk of the
Republican ticket down with him.[33] While Democrats voted in
a "solid block" for Carey, Republican superiority dissolved in
a cauldron of resentment. In limp and maudlin imagery,
quoted in the *Cincinnati Daily Gazette* on October 10, Smith
compared the cooperation between Carey and the Democrats
to the betrayal of Christ by Judas. And again, on October 15,
Smith stated in the *Gazette* that the election was "a shower
bath for the soreheads in the Republican party. . . . The long
reign of the Republican party in the State and in most of the
districts, counties and cities has given it a multitude of soreheads of every kind. . . . Our citizens have seen a canvass
carried on in Hamilton county as if the design was to destroy
the Republican party."

The first, third, and second districts that we have discussed—Toledo, Dayton, Cincinnati—were located in the
northcentral, central and southern parts of the state. In these
districts the two major parties were evenly matched. This encouraged the formation of third parties, for they could play
a deciding vote in any election by destroying the delicate balance between the two established parties. In these circumstances ambitious Republican politicians did not hesitate to
break away from their friends whenever it seemed advan-
tageous for them to do so, or whenever the Republicans refused to gratify their slightest whim or desire. The party put

itself in danger whenever it did not give way to the threats or demands made by these politicians, for they were in a position to injure it seriously by launching an independent movement whenever a political crisis arose.

In northern Ohio the political situation was completely different. There the Republican party was clearly supreme, and party factionalism assumed a different character. In the north, disgruntled Republicans allied themselves with the Democrats rather than attempting to establish third parties. A good example of this occurred in the eighteenth congressional district in Ohio, a northern district that included Cleveland, in the fall of 1864. There, Republican ex-Whigs and ex-Democrats had been suspicious of each other for a long time, despite the nominal allegiance of both groups to the Republican party.[34] Finally, in 1865, this general rivalry developed into an acute crisis. At that time Edwin Cowles, an ex-Democrat who had been appointed postmaster of Cleveland by President Lincoln, was replaced by George Benedict, an ex-Whig. These men were powerful political figures in the district, for George Benedict was editor of the *Cleveland Herald* and Edwin Cowles was editor of the *Cleveland Leader,* both papers that carried a considerable measure of political influence.[35] The *Cleveland Plain Dealer,* the chief organ of the Democratic party in the eighteenth district, lost no time in exploiting the quarrel between Cowles and Benedict. On June 23, 1865, the *Plain Dealer* declared: "It is not altogether improbable, that a powerful and troublesome reaction is about to take place, which, even in Ohio, will resolve the factions of which the Republican party has been composed into their original elements. The old members of the Whig party . . . have, by recent developments, been aroused to a consciousness that more is required of them than they can give without losing their self respect."

Cowles was removed from the position of postmaster upon the orders of President Johnson himself, but this order had actually been contrived by his ex-Whig enemies. Cowles claimed that President Johnson was guided in this action by Rufus Spalding, congressman from the eighteenth district and a close political friend of Benedict. There is some evidence that Cowles was correct, for on July 17, 1865, Spalding wrote to President Johnson: "We are pleased with your appointment here for Post-master in the 18th district."

When Cowles lost his place, he looked upon it as an injury he was required to revenge. Therefore, he formed a group of Republicans known as the "bolters" who opposed the official policy and the official nominees of their own party.[36] In order to make their rebellion even more effective Cowles and his friends actually cooperated with the Democrats in an attempt to elect the Democratic party's candidate for the office of state representative. For example, the Cowles forces circulated a petition, quoted in the *Cleveland Plain Dealer* on September 12, 1865, which stated: "The public welfare will be subserved by the substitution of better men for some of the nominees of the Union party of Cuyahoga county."

George Dangler, the Republican nominee, managed to win the place, but, as a result of the alliance between Cowles and the Democrats, his majority in the district was reduced to less than 200 votes. However, the Democrats in the eighteenth district were quick to seize upon the opportunity to demonstrate the difficulties of their opponents. On October 11, 1865, the *Cleveland Plain Dealer* wrote: "The two wings [Republican] have a passion for hating each other, and we have only seen the beginning of what will become a great war between two factions." For his part, Benedict believed that the split between Republicans in the district had dealt a crippling blow to the party from which it might not recover for a considerable time. Benedict was also quoted by the *Cleveland Herald* on September 21, stating certain Republicans in the district had "swallowed nauseous doses politically."

This feud in the eighteenth congressional district almost resulted in a Republican defeat. Nevertheless, the factions of the party were unable to settle their differences. As a result, further problems arose in 1866. In the autumn of 1866 the Republicans were unable to agree upon their nominee for Congress. Rufus Spalding, the incumbent, was supported by George Benedict and his friends, whereas he was hotly opposed by Cowles and his section of the party. As their own choice for congressman Cowles and his friends supported Richard Parsons, the ex-speaker of the Ohio assembly, and a political ally of Salmon P. Chase.[37] In this instance, in order to secure the victory of his nominee, Benedict sought an alliance with the Democrats. They were prepared to support Spalding in return for a measure of the patronage if he won the election. As far as all the parties were concerned, no principles were involved. In 1865 Cowles had cooperated with the Democrats solely for partisan advantage. In 1866 Benedict performed the same disservice to his party, and for exactly the same reasons. The chief object of all these Republicans was victory, and they desired victory in order to share in those spoils that fell to the victor's lot in the ordinary course of political life in the state, so the *Cleveland Plain Dealer* claimed on June 27, 1866. In fact, each of these two groups of Republicans cooperated with the Democrats in order to enjoy an advantage over the other. The *Cleveland Herald* wrote on June 23, 1866: "The attempt is to be made by the friends of Mr. Parsons to carry the city for that gentleman through the votes of the Copperheads. Prominent Democrats, who never acted with the Union party, are at work all over the city to carry out this scheme. We can give names." For his part, Spalding was fully capable of this same tactic. "You tickle me and I'll tickle you," was the way in which the *Leader* described Spalding's dealings with the Democrats in an article on July 25, 1866. (On the subject of political patronage in Cleveland see Chapter Four.)

The same dismal picture of Republican disunity may be found in the nineteenth congressional district, located in the Western Reserve region of Ohio in the northeast. The chief rivalry in this district lay between John Hutchins, an ex-Whig, and congressman James Garfield. In 1862 Garfield, who was something of a local military hero, was persuaded to challenge Hutchins for the Republican nomination for Congress, and he managed to win the place.[38] Four years later, the bickering between these two Republicans broke out into open warfare when Garfield was renominated. Hutchins, who had conspired for months to prevent this, then joined forces with the Democrats.[39]

Although Hutchins' opposition to Garfield·was largely personal, many of his followers, who were protectionists, were critical of Garfield's advocacy of free trade.[40] Garfield, moreover, had appeared as a defense lawyer in the trial of three Indiana Democrats charged with treason; this action aroused a good deal of opposition to him in his own district.[41] Garfield, with strong support from Lyman Hall, the editor of the *Portage County Democrat,* was reelected, but only after a hard campaign in which he was on the defensive during much of the contest. On the issue of a protective tariff, for example, Garfield wrote to one Republican in his district: "You know my views on the tariff, and I am assailed by the Free Traders and the Extreme Tariff men. My own course is chosen, and it is quite possible that it will throw me out of public life." [42] In 1868 Garfield prevailed again, even though the party was split in the same way that it had been in 1866, but his triumph left Republicans snarling at each other viciously.[43] One of Garfield's supporters crowed, "We have scored a victory over the most vile, low, vulgar standards that was [*sic*] ever put forth in a political campaign." [44]

As these examples suggest, the game of fusion politics, on whatever terms it was played, did not normally make Democrats out of Republicans. The latter preserved their association with the party even when they worked against it. In a speech given in Cincinnati, for example, and reported in the *Cincinnati Daily Gazette* on September 11, 1867, Samuel Carey told his audience: "I am no Democrat, never worked with the Democrats. I have always been a Republican. I will be an independent candidate for office. I am a Republican; I embrace the principles enunciated in the Republican platform. I am as good a Republican as Mr. Smith, and I want the Democrats to understand it that vote for me." This same kind of statement was made by other Independent Republicans as well.

Yet a section of Republicans did join the opposition. The change from Republican to Democrat was neither as illogical nor as difficult to make as it may seem. These "renegades" were not slow to observe that, among voters, loyalty to the Democratic party was remarkably durable; and Democratic leaders could, in most areas of the state depend upon regular support for their party from registered Democrats. Moreover, following the war, the Democrats introduced the practice of nominating ex-Republicans and war veterans to positions of importance in their party. This practice offered exceptional opportunities for the men who took them to move to the front rank of politics without competing with an older generation of Democratic politicians, as would have been the case had they remained within the Republican party.[45]

Politics in Lucas County, Ohio, reflected these general developments to a remarkable degree. In 1865, two of the five candidates on the Democratic ticket were ex-Republicans and two others were ex-Union officers, who had never been active in local politics.[46] Of the five Democratic candidates in 1867, two were ex-Republicans, and one was an ex-Union officer. In 1869, two of the five Democratic candidates were ex-Republicans, and two were ex-Union officers.[47] The *Toledo Blade,* a staunchly Republican paper, called these tickets "mongrel affairs," and accused the "renegade" Republicans who participated in them of sacrificing principle for the sake of office. And a lead editorial in the *Toledo Daily Blade* on October 5, 1868, is typical of the attitude of the Republicans in Lucas County toward this development.

If men are at liberty to say for every cause, however slight, "We belong to the Republican party, but if our views are not met in the selection of candidates we shall vote with the opposite party," they practically belong to that other party. And if they carry that principle of action into that other party, they will be no help to it. There must be a practical, common sense rule observed, or party organizations fall before the pragmatical, capricious judgments of misguided, or perhaps disappointed, factious and selfish men.

This pattern was repeated in almost every congressional district in the state, as may be seen if we investigate the leading Republican newspapers in the state, and even if we investigate a considerable number of county newspapers as well. As the *Cincinnati Daily Gazette* on October 15, 1867, put it: "Every county has its quota." In 1866, six of the nineteen Democrats on the state congressional ticket were ex-Republicans, several of whom had failed to get the nomination from their own party. These men were Durbin Ward, John F. McKinney, William Munger, Thomas Miller, Thomas Commanger, and Louis Schaffer, Democratic candidates for the third, fourth, fifth, seventh, tenth, and seventeenth districts respectively. We should notice that Ward, McKinney, Miller and Commanger had failed to win the Republican nomination for Congress. By 1870, this number had increased to nine, fully one-half of the entire Democratic ticket. These men were Samuel Carey, Lewis Campbell, John McKinney, Charles Lamison, James Hubbell, William Lockwood, Ralph Leete, Lyman Critchfield, and John Ball, Democratic candidates for the first, third, fourth, fifth, eighth, tenth, eleventh, fourteenth, and seventeenth districts respectively. There were, of course, strong objections from veteran Democrats who demanded the nomination of only faithful party workers, but their protests had little, if any, influence.[48]

Every kind of issue and personal rivalry could, upon occasion, have a telling effect on the fortunes of the Republican party in the congressional districts of Ohio during this period.

IV

The divisiveness and rivalries in congressional elections had their counterparts at the state level, particularly for the governor's office. In 1867, the Republican convention nominated Rutherford B. Hayes as the party's candidate for governor, alienating a section of Republicans who had supported Benjamin Cowan.[49] Cowan was the chairman of the Republican State Central Committee. Because his aspirations were thwarted by Hayes, he never forgave him and from that time

on worked to undo him. For one thing, as chairman, Cowan
made sure that the State Central Committee did not function
as it should have during the fall campaign. It should have set
up a speaking schedule, organized local rallies, and coordinated
the campaign in the top echelons of the party; instead it did
almost nothing.[50] Cowan's dereliction aroused the deepest resentment among Hayes's supporters, and privately they condemned his behavior. In the weeks following the election, as
the following statement shows, Republican leaders and William Smith in particular condemned Cowan as a traitor to his
party. "He [Cowan] took the extraordinary course, when he
found Gen. Hayes was a candidate for the nomination before
our convention, of avowing himself his implacable enemy. . . .
he proclaimed through his nearest friend that now he 'should
lay back and go to cutting throats.' " [51] In part, it was Cowan's
foot dragging that caused the Republican party to lose control
of the legislature and to scrape into the governor's office by
less than three thousand votes. A second factor of significance
in the defeat of the Republican party in 1867 was the loss of
a seat in the United States Senate. In 1868 Benjamin F. Wade,
the veteran Republican from Ohio, was faced with reelection
to the Senate. With the Democrats now in control of the Ohio
legislature it was clear that Wade's career in the Senate had
ended.

In the seventh congressional district, which included Columbus, an Independent party opposed the reelection of the
Republican incumbent, Samuel Shellabarger, to Congress in
1866.[52] In the seventeenth congressional district, Republicans
bolted their party in 1865 and again in 1868 to nominate Independent candidates for state and local offices.[53] In the eleventh congressional district, a ramshackle coalition of ex-Republicans, Democrats, and Trade Unionists maintained a separate ticket in the field throughout the decade of the sixties.[54]
The greenback issue of 1867 and 1868 superimposed even
greater confusion on these divisions. A scattering of "People's" parties sprang up all over the state, uniting Republicans and Democrats. Their avowed objective was to have the
war debt paid off in paper money–greenbacks, rather than in

gold, with the intention of inflating the currency. (See Chapter Six.)

It is thus clear that politics in the state of Ohio, so far as the Republicans were concerned, were dynamic, complicated, and treacherous. The appearance of splinter parties and factions in the various districts of the state became almost a commonplace of public life. No Republican could feel certain of the attitude of his fellows. Constantly shifting groups of Republicans sought only immediate advantage, to the neglect of party unity. Sometimes they aligned themselves with the Democrats; sometimes they formed third parties; sometimes they pursued party vendettas of local significance; sometimes they deserted the ranks of their party merely in order to share, however briefly, in the spoils of office.

V

The significance of this grass roots disintegration has generally been overlooked. At the state and national level the line between Republicans and Democrats existed after the war, as before. But at the district and county level and locally, no such rigid line divided the two parties. As we have seen, the process of pulling apart had begun during the war and intensified after it. The basic condition of Republican politics was lack of organization, lack of discipline, fragmentation, and the shiftings of one group to another. As one correspondent described it, the Republican party was "an imaginary party," a figment of rhetoric.[55] Of unified program and ideology, it had little; of organization, still less; only the label remained, and Republicans disagreed even about this.

"We are at an end of parties," Harper's *Weekly* proclaimed in the issue of February 25, 1865, understanding the flux and turmoil rampant in Ohio and elsewhere. This phrase has been used to suggest that, following the war, Republicans found themselves in a position of power and influence such as no party in the country had enjoyed before.[56] Such was not the case, at least in Ohio. The prevailing opinion—the dominant concern—among Ohio Republicans was the possible breakup of the Republican party and the formation of new coalitions. The war was over; old issues were played out; and the diversity of views on political affairs inevitably suggested that new alignments would be formed to cater to these new views and interests. On December 29, 1865, the *Cincinnati Daily Commercial* declared: "He must be of dull perception who does not see that process going on."

As things stood, Republican leaders were wholly unsure of their basis of support and of their majorities. What kind of opposition from within the party might topple them from office? Around what issues might that opposition be raised? What actions might prevent dissident Republicans from bolting the party and forming separate tickets? How might an officeholder enhance his strength in his constituency? James Garfield, it has been said, represented a "safe" district in Congress.[57] Yet he found his position threatened again and again by a nebulous opposition. Various issues elicited various responses: Negro suffrage, protective tariffs, taxation, among others, plagued the lives of the Republican politicians. Each of these issues had its proponents and opponents within the party, encouraging men to use them for their own political purposes. In a letter which one Republican leader prepared for the information of Jacob Cox about the condition of Republican politics we find the following statement: "Aside from your friends and your well deserved reputation, there are currents and under currents in the personal politics of Ohio which may probably find in that direction [business] a more acceptable escape from less agreeable results than in any other way." [58] At times, Garfield despaired of continuing his career in politics; his friends urged him to leave Congress for business, so dangerous and troublesome were the politics of the time. Although Garfield may have represented a "safe" district, so far as his majorities were concerned, his disgust with the factionalism in his party is borne out by a letter which he wrote to Burke Hinsdale, president of Hiram College in 1868. "Before many weeks my immediate political future will be decided. I care less about the result than I have ever cared before." [59]

VI

Into this situation of disruption, demoralization, and personal disagreements, a new kind of Republican politician began to appear, and his emergence was no accident. The very chaos invited men with ambition and purpose and few ties with the past to breathe new spirit into the party, to keep it together, and to give it a new sense of purpose. The story of Republican politics, from this point of view, is the story of new leadership, and a description of the beliefs and attitudes for which it spoke.

The Ohio legislature of 1865 reflects the influx of these new types of Republicans in the party. The great majority of Republican members had never served in the legislature before. From the biographical material that is available to us, incomplete as it must be, it is clear that most of them had few connections with either the Whig or the Democratic party of the prewar period. They were newcomers to both the Republican party and state politics. This is confirmed by a welter of comment to this effect by Republicans themselves. "The men most prominent during a revolution almost invariably sink to the bottom when the revolution is over," Garfield was reminded by a Republican correspondent, one of his chief lieutenants in the district. "The government of the country is destined to go into the hands of a widely different class of men." [60]

One important characteristic which identified this "different class" of Republicans was that they had seen service in the Civil War. They were war veterans; most of them had been commissioned officers, and they realized that their war records placed them in a favorable position over even the most highly placed civilian. As one Republican grumbled, "There is a combination amongst certain officers of the army to monopolize hereafter all civil offices." [61] Another critic of this policy explained the situation in more precise terms: "The politics of this state are run upon a military basis at present, which I suppose will hereafter be much the case everywhere.

The best offices have become the prize and reward of military service." [62]

Service in the Union army was a valuable training ground for politics. It introduced men to discipline, responsibility, and corporate loyalty; it also bridged the gulf between the worlds of private and public affairs, for officers were called upon to make speeches, raise enlistments, and bolster enthusiasm for the war effort. Moreover, it required men to exercise a wide range of administrative powers unknown to them before: the supervision of elections, the planning of military tactics, and the care and conduct of personnel. Their army experience, in short, was a form of vocational training in political and administrative responsibility, and these men carried their training back with them into civilian life.

In his *Reminiscences,* for example, Jacob Cox wrote of the Civil War:

> A man wholly without business training would always be in embarrassment, though his other qualifications for military life were good. Even a company has a good deal of administrative business to do. Accounts are to be kept, rations, clothing. . . . Returns of various kinds are to be made, applications, musters, rolls and the like. It was a very rare thing for a man of middle age to make a good company officer. It was astonishing to see the rapidity with which well educated and earnest young men progressed. They quickly grasped the principles of their new profession, and made themselves masters of tactics and administrative duties. . . . Lawyers in this respect, were most helpful. They called meetings, addressed the people to raise enthusiasm, urged enlistments.[63]

Nor did the new Republicans monopolize only the "best offices" in the party. At the district and county levels, and locally, their claim on political office was virtually complete. In the past, local papers had described the candidates of the party as "ex-Whigs" or "ex-Democrats," but now the description changed to "ex-Union officers" or else "young men." Occasionally, as in Scioto County, the Republican ticket was called simply "the military slate." [64] In 1865 four of the six Republicans on the party ticket in Jefferson County, for example, were ex-Union officers. None of these men had ever held a political office before; it would not be difficult to reproduce this pattern for almost every county in the state.

This practice was not endorsed by all Republicans. Many Republicans who had remained at home during the war were always irritated and often angered and aroused by the favoritism shown to the military candidates—the "empty sleeve policy," as it came to be called. Thus in Jefferson County a resolution was moved, though it failed of adoption, that only Republicans who had served the party in the past should be nominated for office.[65] In fact, the empty sleeve policy prompted some Republicans to leave the party and join ranks with the Democrats in disgust at the opposition offered them by the Republican Old Guard.

Among the most successful of the new Republicans were James A. Garfield, Jacob D. Cox, Isaac Sherwood, Warren Keifer, Rutherford B. Hayes, Aaron F. Perry, and Edward F. Noyes.[66] In many ways they may be considered representative of the others. All were young. Cox was 37 when he became governor of the state. Hayes was 45 and Noyes 39 when elected to the same office. Garfield was only 32 when he succeeded Joshua P. Giddings in Congress. When the war ended their average age was 33. By contrast, Republicans who had been among the founders of the party were a generation older. Benjamin F. Wade was 65, Thomas Ewing 76, Rufus Spalding 67, and Thomas Corwin 69. Within a few years many of these veteran Republicans either had died, or retired from politics, or had been beaten out of public life by the vigorous ex-soldiers who sought yet further laurels in the politics of their state. The new Republicans were not drawn from any one social class. Most of them were the sons of families that had migrated to the Ohio frontier in the early nineteenth century. Nearly all received formal education to a level far above the average for the age. Garfield was educated at Williams College, Hayes at Kenyon, Cox at Oberlin, and Noyes at Antioch. Most of them became lawyers; others, like Murat Halstead, James Comly, Whitelaw Reid, and William Henry Smith, went into journalism. They moved easily from college into a profession, often to relatively high positions. This background of education, comfort, and rapid promotion was very different from that of the older Republicans, like Benjamin Wade. Wade had been born of a poor family, was self-educated, and studied law while working at various occupations.[67]

As young, aspiring professional men, the new Republicans were attracted to the cities—Cleveland, Cincinnati, Toledo— small towns in the 1830s which had mushroomed into large commercial centers. The city, like the new Republicans themselves, appeared as the source for all that was vital and energetic and progressive in society. "Push, labor, shove," Hayes wrote to his mother from Cincinnati, "these words are of great power in a city like this." [68]

They were city men by temperament and by profession. The city was their frontier; it expanded their horizons, for it freed them, as Garfield said, from "the shell of local notions." [69] They were excited by its variety and vitality—the hum of industry stirred them, visions of unending growth filled their eyes. "Is there a limit to the progress of society?" Hayes asked rhetorically. They delighted in the nascent culture of city life, and contrasted it to the "dreary" wasteland of rural Ohio, from which many of them had fled.[70]

At the beginning of the war the new Republicans had joined the Union army as commissioned officers. Many of them had harbored political ambitions prior to the war, but the war itself catapulted them into political office. Hayes, Garfield, and Schenck were elected to Congress during the war; others assumed political office just after it ended. Cox was elected governor in 1865. Willard Warner, Edward Parrott, William Steedman, and Benjamin Eggleston were elected to the state legislature in the same year.

They were swiftly disillusioned after assuming political office. They discovered that the bickering among Republicans made a mockery of the name of their party. They joined the party as it was entering the stage of profound dissolution. As

we have indicated, the party contained large elements con-
sisting of men who spoke for ideals of a most reactionary
nature; others were anxious to further some special cause,
and most simply wanted to enjoy the support of their own
political followers.[71] One Republican described the political
condition in Ohio in the following way:

> The party formations thus far seem . . . too indefinite.
> They lack marrow, root, genius, energy on the part of
> their representatives, originality in their principles.
> Our Democrats were not copperhead enough, and our
> "Radicals" too conservative, too unrevolutionary. And
> between the conservatives and radicals drifted, like the
> eyes in a plate of rice soup, the hybrid party of repub-
> lican phillisters; Scribes and Pharisees, that belonged
> to neither, but like the thief in the night made off with
> the booty, while "copperheads" and "radicals" were
> pulling each other's ears.

The party, in fact, was a battleground of warring factions,
with each directly opposed to the other on many vital subjects
of government. "Everyone talks about the need for party
unity," Cox reported in 1865, yet "we do not hestitate to cut
each others' throats in perfect contempt of all unity when the
advantage of a part of the party may be found in it." [72]

The new Republicans thought of politics in different
terms. To them, party politics was a "specialty" and, like any
special concern, it needed careful attention, organization and,
above all, strict discipline.[73] In practice, this meant the substitution of unified action for personal independence; consoli-
dation would have to take precedence over decentralization.
They compared this approach with the administrative methods
of large business corporations. Later, they proposed various
"reforms" which would make their party more "businesslike"
and efficient: the creation of a State Executive Committee
with enough power to exert its authority in rural counties as
well as in isolated hamlets, in populous centers as well as in
city wards; the nomination of candidates for state and na-

tional office at the district rather than county level; the abolition of the open primary; and a "test oath" which would com-
pel Republicans to declare their allegiance to the party and
respect its decisions.[74] These "reforms," the new Republicans
explained, were not intended merely to ensure the political
success of the party. They genuinely believed that new methods were needed in order to serve the best interests of the
community. In the place of the haphazard practices of the
past, they wanted centralization, discipline, and the rigorous
organization of their party's affairs. As a result, they felt, the
Republicans could achieve all those things that were the requirements of a more advanced and more sophisticated society
of the kind that was now emerging in the period following
the war.[75]

The new Republicans' disillusionment with their party
went deeper than that caused by its lack of organization. They
were also critical of the party leadership. They found this
leadership inadequate, a feeling that came naturally to those
who wanted to lead. A good deal of power lay in the hands
of men who had spent their entire political careers on the
issue of Negro slavery. The slavery problem had been the
basis upon which these men had built their authority and
achieved their positions in the party. But the war had solved
that problem. Slavery was abolished, and it seemed obvious
to the new Republicans that the reason for the hegemony of
these men was over. The attitude of William D. Howells reflected the opinion of these new Republicans toward the older
generation of Republican leaders. Howells wrote of Benjamin
F. Wade: "It was Wade's misfortune to outlive the period
when the political struggle with slavery passed into the Civil
War, and to carry into that the spirit of an earlier time, with
his fierce alienation from the patient policy of Lincoln, and
his espousal of the exaggerations of Reconstruction." [76]

The war had ushered in a new era and the new times
brought with them strange requirements. Both the nation and
the Republican party had to move forward in order to face
national problems of a novel and unprecedented kind. In order
to deal with them successfully statesmen would find it neces-

sary to master all those developments that in combination were producing a period of unparalleled economic growth. After 1865 the scope of things had changed. As a result, party politicians would now have to concern themselves with such issues as national banking practices, a national currency, immense new railroad systems, and all those other factors that together were creations of an industrial, urban community in the place of the frontier society that had existed before.

After 1865, in just a few years, these men gradually took on an identity of their own. They were called Republicans of the "younger set" and "progressives." [77] They had taken no part in those events that led to the outbreak of the Civil War, and for this reason they felt themselves qualified to interpret what the North's victory in the war could mean for the future of the whole country.

This sense of identity did not mean that these "new Republicans" acted in concert as a separate group within the party. They often disagreed on a variety of personal, political, and economic issues, but they were marked off from other Republicans by their unity of purpose and the vigor of their actions on behalf of the party. They were first and foremost Republicans—not ex-Whigs or ex-Democrats or the members of one faction or another who were never able to give wholehearted allegiance to the Republican party for its own sake.

If the new Republicans were different, it was in their ideas and attitudes about the future. The basis of their drive for power was the belief that the party needed new leaders, and the leaders needed a new faith, which was to be found in cities, in factories, in railroads. And here they broke with party veterans like Benjamin Wade, who belonged to an older and different kind of America, which was passing. "Such men as you must do it. Young, ambitious, and enthusiastic. You must do it. Wade can't," Garfield was told by his friends who desired a change in the leadership of the party.[78]

VII

The new Republicans realized they had joined a disintegrating party and saw more clearly than the others the need for a rallying cry that could unite the party in the eyes of the public. The term "radical," which had belonged to the old antislavery Republicans, was now adopted by the new Republicans.[79] Three things about this term must be made clear. First, the term itself was not simply an epithet foisted on Republicans by the Democrats. Second, it was used by the new Republicans to project an image of the party for public consumption. Third, each group of Republicans in the party had its own private interpretation of the term.

The word "radical" had been used by Republicans to refer to themselves—and by their opponents—for over a decade. It had first been applied to that group of antislavery zealots who formed the nucleus of the party in the midfifties. In 1864, however, "radicalism" referred to a different group, a group of Republicans, known as the "radicals," who were boldly opposed to Lincoln's renomination for office. (The immediate cause of their revolt was the military failure of the North. Lincoln also supported a reconstruction policy for the South which these Republicans found unacceptable.) [80]

It is necessary to keep these facts in mind while considering the use of the word "radical" in the period after 1865. The Democrats flung the word at Republicans for propaganda purposes, at that time, to imply that the Republican party was engaged in a "plot" to fasten Negro suffrage on the nation and to establish military rule over the South.[81] Differences existed among Republicans over a reconstruction program for the South, and the motive of the Democrats was clear. They hoped to inflame Republican passions and involve their opponents in a major political dispute that would break their party into pieces.

Jacob Cox, for his part, looked upon this tactic with fear and apprehension. On July 30, 1865, he wrote to Garfield:

Each day shows more clearly the tactics of the Copperheads and that they are having a certain degree of
success. They are at work, quietly or diligently, in all
the counties, especially in the southern part of the
state, meeting the soldiers as they return home and ap-
proaching them with appeals to the personal prejudice
against the negro. They tell them that the issue is to be
forced upon them whether they will share all social and
political privileges with the slaves, and that the only
way to avoid such a result is to return to the bosom of
the Democracy.

But the common currency which the epithet gained was
not entirely due to Democratic efforts. The new Republicans
responded by taking the epithet to themselves and disarming
the fears which the Democrats were trying to arouse. "Don't
let the Democrats alarm you," was the reply of these Republicans. "We are radicals, but only in our desire to move ahead in
peace and security and to stand in the vanguard of progress." [82]
This was an effective way of turning aside Democratic propaganda. It also cast a blanket of innocence over the genuinely
extreme proposals that came from some members of their own
party. This type of "radicalism" committed Republicans to no
specific program. It did identify the party in the public mind
with vague and undefined ideas of progress, energy, and the
ability to deal with the problems of the future in a novel and
untraditional way.

The very vagueness of this program was studiously culti-
vated by the new Republicans, who were most aware of the
party's deficiencies. Even so, this "radical" image was not
simply the product of political cynicism, for it fitted, if rather
loosely, the young Republicans' expectations of the future.

Several groups within the Republican party fastened the
label "radical" upon themselves, but all of them had different
views of what the term meant or implied. Each of these factions accepted the term as they defined it themselves, and rejected the definitions of every other group. The younger Republicans, for example, accepted the term in their own sense

of it, but they were very critical of other "radicals" in their party. They rejected the "radicalism" of those rebellious Republicans who promoted policies that might lead to internal party strife. And these Republicans, in their turn, were opposed to the "radicalism" of the young men who were different from them, and therefore suspect. We may conclude therefore that radicalism was at best a very delicate web holding these groups together—an adhesive concept, to be sure, but one that was as fragile as it was intricate. The term served in some measure as a blanket to hide the structural weaknesses of the party from the public at large, but it did nothing at all to cure them.

VIII

As we have seen, the political successes of the Republicans during the war years inaccurately reflected the confused condition of their party. On one level, a vertical division between ex-Whigs and ex-Democrats expressed itself in bitter factional quarrels, third party movements, and outright losses to the Democrats. In 1865 Republicans blamed themselves as much as the Democrats for the fact that the party had done so poorly in the state elections in Ohio. A horizontal division between generations also developed soon after the war. As time passed, especially during the next few years, the younger Republicans came more and more to regard their veteran colleagues as the major disruptive element in the fortunes of the party. These leaders, representing the differing factions of the party, all realized that their chronic disunity would bedevil any search for solutions to the highest national problems. For these reasons Republicans in Ohio, despite what historians have said about the strength of the party in 1865, looked forward to the future with feelings of grave anxiety and even dismay.

NOTES

1. For voting returns in Ohio, in both state and national elections, see Joseph Smith, *The Republican Party in Ohio* (Chicago, 1898), pp. 39–278.

2. Lewis D. Campbell to D. P. Patterson, January 22, 1866, *Andrew Johnson mss.*, Library of Congress.

3. The divisions between the various factions in the Republican party in the prewar period are examined in David Potter, *Lincoln and His Party During the Secession Crisis* (New Haven, 1942), pp. 40–52.

4. In this connection see Reinhard H. Luthin, "Salmon P. Chase's Political Career Before the Civil War," *Mississippi Valley Historical Review*, Vol. XXIV (1942–1943), *passim;* Joseph Rayback, "The Liberty Party Leaders of Ohio: Exponents of Anti-Slavery Coalition," *Ohio State Archaeological and Historical Society Quarterly*, LVII (1948), 165–72; Albert Riddle, "The Election of Salmon P. Chase to the Senate," *The Republic*, IV (1875), 179–83. The ambition of Chase in 1860 is discussed in Donnal V. Smith, "Salmon P. Chase and the Election of 1860," *Ohio Archaeological and Historical Publications*, XXIX (1930), 512–25; Earl W. Wiley, "Governor John Greiner and Chase's Bid for the Presidency in 1860," *Ohio State Archaeological and Historical Society Quarterly*, LVIII (1949), 251–56.

5. Elizabeth F. Yager, "The Presidential Campaign of 1864 in Ohio," *Ohio State Archaeological and Historical Society Quarterly*, XXXIV (1925), 552–53; Charles R. Wilson, "The Original Chase Meeting and the Next Presidential Election," *Mississippi Valley Historical Review*, XXIII (1936), 61–79; William F. Zornow, "Lincoln, Chase, and the Ohio Radicals in 1864," *Bulletin of the Historical and Philosophical Society of Ohio*, IX (1954), 4, 14.

6. For a discussion of the political battles between the Whigs and the Democrats in the years before the formation of the Republican party see Eugene A. Holt, *Party Politics in Ohio, 1840–1850* (Columbus, 1944), pp. 107–55. The hostility of the ex-Democrats toward the ex-Whigs is expressed in Alphonso Taft to Benjamin F. Wade, September 8, 1864, *Benjamin F. Wade mss.*, Library of Congress; *Portage County Democrat*, February 23, 1865; *The Loraine County News*, June 23, 1865; *The Mahoning Register*, July 12, 1865; *The Cleveland Leader*, June 25, 1865.

7. For this quotation and the attacks of Republicans like Howells upon political "opportunism" see William D. Howells to William C. Howells in Mildred Howells (ed.), *Life and Letters of William Dean Howells* (New York, 1928), p. 26; William Dean Howells, *Years of My Youth* (New York, 1916), pp. 147–48.

8. For a discussion of the differences between Democrats upon the issue of the war see Charles R. Wilson, "The *Cincinnati Daily Enquirer* and Civil War Politics: A Study in Copperhead Opinion" (unpublished

Ph.D. dissertation, Department of History, University of Chicago, 1937), *passim.*

9. See Eric L. McKitrick, *Andrew Johnson and Reconstruction* (Chicago, 1960), pp. 42–47.

10. A detailed account of the "peace movement" in Ohio is found in Elbert Benton, "The Movement for Peace Without Victory During the Civil War," *Western Reserve Historical Society Collections*, No. 99 (Cleveland, 1918), *passim;* Frank Clement, *The Copperheads of the Middle West* (Chicago, 1961), pp. 201–41.

11. For the opposition of some Democrats in Ohio to the peace movement see Samuel Cox to Manton Marble, March 3, 1865, *Manton Marble mss.*, Library of Congress; George Morgan to George McClellan, March 25, 1864, *George McClellan mss.*, Library of Congress.

12. R. Stephenson to William H. Smith, March 15, 1865, *William Henry Smith mss.*, Ohio Historical Society.

13. Whitelaw Reid, *Ohio in the War* (New York, 1868), pp. 52–63. For Tod's early career in Ohio politics see Delmar J. Trester, "David Tod and the Gubernatorial Campaign of 1844," *Ohio State Archaeological and Historical Society Quarterly*, LXII (1953), 163–67.

14. Edward Noyes to William Smith, May 10, 1865, *William Henry Smith mss.*, Indiana Historical Society; Rush Sloane to Sherman, May 19, 1865, *Sherman mss.; Cleveland Plain Dealer*, May 2, 1865; *Portage County Democrat*, June 2, 1865.

15. Brough's letter may be found in the *Cincinnati Daily Gazette*, June 5, 1865; *Dayton Journal*, June 10, 1865.

16. For the anger of Republican leaders over the factionalism in their party see Aaron Perry to Jacob D. Cox, May 29, June 4, 1865, *Jacob D. Cox mss.*, Oberlin College Library.

17. For a review of Ashley's career in Ohio politics see Maxine B. Kahn, "Congressman Ashley in the Post–Civil War Years," *Northwest Ohio Quarterly*, XXXVI (1964), 118–25.

18. See Thomas Elluth to Charles Kay, October 1, 1866; the *Toledo Daily Blade*, October 2, 1866.

19. See Bruce R. Trimble, *Chief Justice Waite, Defender of the Public Interest* (Princeton, 1938), pp. 67–69; Peter C. Magrath, *Morrison R. Waite, The Triumph of Character* (New York, 1963), pp. 66–70; Clark Waggoner, *History of the City of Toledo* (New York, 1888), pp. 350–51.

20. See, for example, James G. Randall, *The Civil War and Reconstruction* (Boston, 1961), pp. 456–61; T. Harry Williams, *Lincoln and the Radicals* (Madison, 1960), pp. 240–42. For a discussion of anti-Negro prejudice as the most important cause of the Republican defeat in 1862, see V. Jacqui Voegeli, "The Northwest and the Race Issue, 1861–1862," *Mississippi Valley Historical Review*, Vol. L (1963), *passim.*

21. For an analysis of the 1864 presidential campaign in Ohio, see Elizabeth Yager, *The Presidential Campaign of 1864 in Ohio* (Columbus, 1925), *passim;* William F. Zornow, "The Attitude of the Western Reserve on the Re-Election of Lincoln," *Lincoln Herald*, V (1948), 35–39.

22. For the opposition in Ohio to MacLean and other "peace Democrats" see John M. Connell to Thomas Ewing, May 29, 1865, John M.

Connell to Thomas Ewing, Jr., June 14, 1866, *Ewing Family mss.*, Ohio Historical Society; Samuel Cox to Marble, March 3, 1865, *Marble mss.*

23. The Independents in Ashley's district were powerfully aided by Clark Waggoner, editor of the *Toledo Commercial*. For the continued opposition to Ashley's leadership see the editorials of the *Toledo Commercial* in the *Toledo Daily Blade*, June 19–August 23, October 11, November 27, 1866.

24. The proceedings of this convention appeared in the *Toledo Daily Blade*, August 23, 1866.

25. *Dayton Journal*, August 13, 14, 1865; *Dayton Journal*, September 13, 1865.

26. *Dayton Journal*, August 14, 1865; see also *Dayton Journal*, September 13, 15, 1865.

27. For the results of the 1865 election in Montgomery County see *Dayton Journal*, October 13, 1865.

28. *Cincinnati Daily Commercial*, December 23, 28, 29, 30, 1865. Murat Halstead was a close political friend of John Sherman and Salmon Chase. Some Republicans in the second district believed that Halstead planned to use the power and influence of this "new" party in the political interests of both of these Republican leaders. See, in this connection, *Cincinnati Daily Gazette*, December 26, 1865, January 3, 5, 8, 20, 1866.

29. See, for example, J. G. Doddridge to Sherman, January 6, 1866, *Sherman mss.; Cincinnati Daily Gazette*, January 20, 1866; *Miami Union*, December 30, 1865.

30. The complete proceedings of the Workingmen's convention appeared in the *Cincinnati Daily Gazette*, September 13, 1867.

31. See *Cincinnati Daily Gazette*, August 10, 1867, for the proceedings of the Republican convention.

32. For Carey's appeal to urban workers in Cincinnati see *Cincinnati Daily Gazette*, September 11, 13, 1867. Carey's credentials as a "champion" of labor were attacked by Richard Smith in a series of speeches in Cincinnati. See *Cincinnati Daily Gazette*, September 19, 21, 23, 25, 1867.

33. The results of this election appeared in the *Cincinnati Daily Gazette*, October 2, 1867.

34. The conflicts between Republican ex-Whigs and Democrats in Northern Ohio are dealt with in Mary E. Lands, "Old Backbone: Bluff Ben Wade" (unpublished Ph.D. dissertation, Department of History, Western Reserve University, 1957). See also *Cleveland Plain Dealer*, June 23, 1865.

35. *Cleveland Plain Dealer*, June 20, July 17, 1865; *Cleveland Leader*, July 17, 1865; *Cleveland Herald*, June 22, 1865; *Cincinnati Daily Gazette*, July 29, 1865.

36. In this connection see *Cincinnati Daily Gazette*, August 6, 1865.

37. See *Summit County Beacon*, June 2, 1866; *Portage County Democrat*, June 20, 1866; *Cincinnati Daily Gazette*, June 9, 1866.

38. See Theodore Clarke Smith, *The Life and Letters of James Abram Garfield*, I (New Haven, 1925), 225, 234–35.

39. See, in this connection, *Portage County Democrat*, June 20, 1866;

Ashtabula Telegraph, June 23, 1866; *Cleveland Herald,* June 23, 1866; *Mahoning Courier,* June 25, 1866.

40. W. J. Ford to James A. Garfield, May 6, 1866, *James Garfield mss.,* Library of Congress; *Mahoning Courier,* June 20, 1866; *Portage County Democrat,* June 20, 1866.

41. Jacob Cox to Garfield, May 4, 1866, Harmon Austin to Garfield, May 30, 1866; *Garfield mss.; Portage County Democrat,* July 11, 1866.

42. Garfield to Burke Hinsdale, January 1, 1866, quoted in Mary L. Hinsdale (ed.), *Garfield-Hinsdale Letters: Correspondence between James Garfield and Burke Aaron Hinsdale* (Ann Arbor, 1949), p. 73.

43. V. E. Smally to Garfield, June 18, 1868, *Garfield mss.; Mahoning Courier,* May 6, 1868.

44. For this quotation and further information about Garfield's difficulties in 1868 see F. Kinsmen to Garfield, June 26, 1868, H. R. Hall to Garfield, July 6, 1868, E. N. Smally to Garfield, June 1, 1868, *Garfield mss.*

45. This significant aspect of Northern politics in the years following the Civil War has been overlooked by students of that period in American history. In particular, recent writers who have sought to demonstrate the "political supremacy" of the Republican party do less than justice to the highly unstable condition of politics at the local level. In this connection, see McKitrick, *op. cit.,* pp. 46–49.

46. See the Democratic ticket in Lucas County in *Toledo Daily Blade,* August 15, 1865. Biographical material is provided for each candidate on the ticket.

47. See the Democratic ticket in 1867 and 1869 in *Toledo Daily Blade,* September 25, 1867, September 21, 1869.

48. These objections were raised at nearly every Democratic convention. See, for example, *The Crisis,* August 22, 1866; *Steubenville Herald,* May 31, 1867; *Dayton Journal,* August 29, 1867.

49. William Smith to S. S. Knowles, April 27, 1866, Smith to Joseph Barrett, June 6, 1867, *Smith mss.; Dayton Journal,* June 8, 1867.

50. Smith to Samuel Reed, September 13, 1867, Smith to Murat Halstead, October 2, 1861, *Smith mss.; Cincinnati Daily Commercial,* August 1, 1867; *Columbus State Journal,* August 3, 1867.

51. Smith to Gen. Schneider, November 2, 1867, *Smith mss.;* see also Smith to Joseph Mussey, October 27, 1867, *Smith mss.*

52. *Columbus State Journal,* August 31, 1866; *Cincinnati Daily Gazette,* August 7, 1866; *Cleveland Plain Dealer,* September 26, 1866.

53. Benjamin F. Potts to Sherman, May 27, 1866, *Sherman mss.; Steubenville Weekly Herald,* July 19, October 4, 1867; *Cleveland Plain Dealer,* September 26, 1866; *Steubenville Weeky Herald,* May 15, 1868.

54. *The Portsmouth Times,* August 4, 11, 1866, September 21, 1867, April 11, 1868.

55. E. B. Sadler to Sherman, February 28, 1866, *Sherman mss.* See also, in this connection, Jacob Cox to Sherman, January 27, 1866, Durbin Ward to Sherman, January 5, 1867, *Sherman mss.* In a letter to James Garfield, typical of many such expressions, one Republican newspaper editor wrote: "It seems to me, we are today a party of disintegrations." Lyman Hall to Garfield, June 8, 1866, *Garfield mss.*

56. McKitrick, *op. cit.*, pp. 47–48.

57. For example, David Donald includes Garfield among those Republicans who were consistently returned to Congress by their constituents with large majorities. See David Donald, *The Politics of Reconstruction, 1863–1867* (Baton Rouge, 1965), p. 37.

58. Aaron F. Perry to Jacob Cox, May 29, 1865, *Jacob D. Cox mss.*, Oberlin College Library. In this connection, see also William Painter to Sherman, August 30, 1865, *Sherman mss.;* Smith to Joseph Barrett, June 6, 1867, *Smith mss.;* Cox to Garfield, July 30, 1865, *Garfield mss.*

59. Garfield to Burke Hinsdale, March 8, 1868 in Hinsdale, *op. cit.*, p. 132.

60. C. H. Hill to Garfield, March 17, 1867, *Garfield mss.*

61. For this quotation and additional statements of a similar nature see Edward Noyes to Smith, May 10, 1865, *Smith mss.;* M. P. Gaddis to Sherman, June 3, 1866, *Sherman mss.;* Jacob Cox to Garfield, July 19, 1865, *Garfield mss.*

62. William Furay to Smith, June 12, 1865, *Smith mss.*

63. Jacob D. Cox, *Military Reminiscences of the Civil War*, I (New York, 1900), 169–70.

64. *Miami Union*, September 2, 1865.

65. See the proceedings of the Jefferson County Republican convention in the *Steubenville Weekly Herald*, August 30, 1865.

66. For biographies of these new Republican leaders see Robert Caldwell, *James A. Garfield: Party Chieftain* (New York, 1931); Theodore C. Smith, *James Abram Garfield: The Life and Letters* (New Haven, 1925); H. J. Eckenrode, *Rutherford B. Hayes: Statesman of Reunion* (New York, 1930), Harry Barnard, *Rutherford B. Hayes and His America* (Indianapolis, 1954); William C. Cochran, *Political Experiences of Major General Jacob D. Cox* (Cincinnati, 1940); Edgar L. Gray, "The Career of William H. Smith, Politician-Journalist" (unpublished Ph.D. dissertation, Department of History, Ohio State University, 1950).

67. The best biography on Wade is by Hans L. Trefousse, *Benjamin Franklin Wade: Radical Republican from Ohio* (New York, 1963).

68. Hayes to Fanny Hayes, September 23, 1849, in Charles R. Williams (ed.), *Diary and Letters of Rutherford B. Hayes* (Columbus, 1922), pp. 271–72.

69. Garfield to Margaret Rudolph, July 30, 1855, *ibid.*, p. 73; Garfield to Mary Fuller, July 30, 1855, *ibid.*, pp. 79–80; Garfield to Burke Hinsdale, January 10, 1859, *ibid.*, p. 147; James R. Ewing, *Public Services of Jacob D. Cox* (Washington, 1893), p. 8.

70. Hayes to Sardis Birchard, July 29, 1839, *ibid.*, p. 270; Garfield to Margaret Rudolph, October 24, 1857, *ibid.*, pp. 110–11.

71. Garfield to Burke Hinsdale, January 22, 1860, *ibid.*, pp. 144–46; Aaron F. Perry to Cox, June 4, 1865, Cox to William Dennison, July 9, 1865, *Cox mss.*

72. Jacob Cox to Charles Cox, August 7, 1865, *Cox mss.*

73. John Sherman to William Sherman, October 24, 1862, *William Sherman mss.*, Library of Congress; Smith to Whitelaw Reid, June 5, 1865, *Smith mss.; Cincinnati Daily Commercial*, June 23, 1865.

74. See *Cincinnati Daily Gazette,* October 23, 1866; *Miami Union,* September 1, 1866; *Dayton Journal,* June 27, 1867.

75. Richard Smith to Warner Bateman, December 29, 1864, *Warner Bateman mss.,* Western Reserve University; James Stanley to Isaac Strohm, January 23, 1865, *Isaac Strohm mss.,* Ohio Historical Society; Henry Cooke to John Sherman, June 27, 1865, *John Sherman mss.*

76. Howells, *op. cit.,* p. 109.

77. See, for example, Simon Nash to John Sherman, January 12, 1866, Nash to Sherman, January 24, 1866, A. Denny to Sherman, January 17, 1866, *Sherman mss.*

78. E. B. Taylor to Garfield, December 21, 1864.

79. For a discussion of the "radicalism" of the "original" members of the Republican party see McKitrick, *op. cit.,* pp. 53–66.

80. For a discussion of Lincoln's plan of reconstruction and the reaction of the "radicals" to it see Williams, *op. cit.,* pp. 317–23.

81. See, for example, *The Cincinnati Daily Enquirer,* July 28, August 17, September 27, 1865.

82. See the editorials on this point in the *Cincinnati Daily Gazette,* September 19, 1865; *Coshocton Age,* July 21, 1865; *The Weekly Steubenville Herald,* July 12, 1865.

The Party Finds a Policy

CHAPTER TWO

I

When the Civil War ended in 1865 the nation's statesmen brooded over two general problems of vital significance for the future of the entire country. It was obvious to all, even the most partisan Northerners, that sooner or later the South would have to be readmitted into the Union and its people represented in the national Congress. At the same time it was clear, even to the most bitter Southerners, that some provision would have to be made to protect the four million Negroes in the Southern states, all ex-slaves, in their new-found freedom. Even before the war ended men had begun to ponder those political rights and privileges which might be granted these Negroes in the postwar period. Of course, these two problems affected one another very closely, but for the purposes of our analysis it will be useful for us to deal with them separately in order to make clear exactly what was involved in each of them.

On May 29, 1865, President Johnson issued two procla-

41

mations which were to serve as the basis upon which the Southern states would be readmitted into the Union. The first of these was a Proclamation of Amnesty and the second was the Proclamation on North Carolina.[1]

The amnesty proclamation promised pardon to all those who would take an oath of allegiance to the United States. There were certain exceptions to this general rule. President Lincoln had earlier established a number of categories of ex-Confederates who were to be refused a pardon. It was now decided to include within these categories men with taxable property of over $20,000. By the terms of the proclamation these men, along with the other excluded classes of ex-Confederates, were required to make a special application for executive pardon, which might be granted by the President at his discretion.

In the Proclamation on North Carolina President Johnson gave some public expression to his scheme of reconstruction. The proclamation appointed a provisional governor whose duty it was "at the earliest practicable period" to call a convention to be chosen by the loyal people of the state. Loyalty was defined as willingness to take the oath prescribed in the amnesty proclamation. The convention was to draw up a new constitution which would prescribe voting and office-holding qualifications and also provide for a republican form of government for the state. During this interim period executive authority in the state was to be exercised by a "provisional governor." His supreme task, aided by the military, was to begin the process by which North Carolina would prepare itself to resume its normal relations with the Union.[2]

This Proclamation on North Carolina became the model upon which the readmission of the other Southern states was based. In his later pronouncements, however, the President insisted upon certain further conditions requiring the Southern states to nullify their ordinances of secession, to repudiate their Confederate war debts, and to ratify the Thirteenth Amendment abolishing slavery.

When the objectives of the convention had been achieved, elections would be held for the state legislature and also for a governor. Once a governor was elected he would take the place of the provisional governor. At the same time delegates would be chosen by the people of each state who would, in their turn, seek admittance to the Congress of the United States as representatives.

By the end of 1865 every Southern state except Texas had complied with these provisions, and their delegates to Congress waited in Washington to take their seats when Congress reconvened. As far as President Johnson was concerned, the reconstruction of the South had been achieved.

For Republican members of Congress, however, the business was far from settled. In the first place, they believed that Johnson's program had proceeded too rapidly, and that their dignity and pride as congressmen had been impugned by his failure to seek their advice.[3] Several prominent Republican congressional leaders had grave doubts about the practicability of his program. During the early summer, they called on Johnson and he gave them a hearing. However, they found their interviews singularly unsatisfying, for it seemed to them all that the President and the leader of their party had no genuine interest in their suggestions, whatever their merits or demerits were. Later on, his refusal to change his course naturally tended to confirm this impression. It seemed that congressional authority, the highest legislative authority in the nation, had been summarily flouted.

In consequence, at the Republican Ohio State Convention in June, 1865, a group of delegates sponsored the following resolution: "Resolved, That it is the belief of this Convention that the reconstruction of the revolted States constitutionally belongs to the Legislative Department of our government, and that the Executive can only provide Provisional Military Governments until such time as Congress may act." (The proceedings of this convention were reported in the *Dayton Journal*, June 23, 1865.)

In the second place, Republican congressmen resented the fact that under the terms of Johnson's policy the Southern states might be admitted into the Union with more seats and more power than they had before they left the Union.[4] Before the war, state representation in Congress was dependent upon the whole number of white adults and three-fifths of the Negroes. After the abolishment of slavery, however, the constitutional reckoning of a Negro as three-fifths of a white was set aside in favor of a full representational value. Under this new dispensation, the South gained twelve additional seats in the House of Representatives—a handsome increase in power for a region that had just been defeated.

In the third place, Johnson's program left a hiatus with regard to the Negro's civil and political rights. Much was made of the fact that he had virtually ignored this subject in his North Carolina proclamation.[5]

Congressional Republicans felt that the latter question could not be ignored, although they themselves were divided over a solution to it. The price of supporting full equality for the Negro could be a high one, for color prejudice had woven itself deep into the fabric of Northern as well as Southern society.[6] Most Republicans rallied behind a vague proposal known as "impartial suffrage" which asked that all voting requirements adopted by the states be applied equally to white and black. Others supported Negro suffrage in the South, but not in the North. Only a handful of Republicans supported universal suffrage. (See Chapter Three.)

In this connection it must be remembered that Congress did not meet until December, 1865. The five months which elapsed between the promulgation of the North Carolina proclamation and the opening of Congress has been largely ignored by historians because in this interim period there was not so much stormy debate on the national level. Yet, as we shall show, it was in these intervening months that the problems of reconstruction and their possible solutions were thrashed out during violent disputes that took place on the level of local politics.

During the early summer of 1865 most Republicans in Ohio avoided a discussion of President Johnson's program. This attitude was followed by one of cautious disapproval, and then by open debate along lines determined not so much by national as by local considerations and conditions. In the end, these Republicans arrived at their own solutions which clashed with the President's measures but which, they believed, would be in the best interests of their party in the localities.

In May, 1865, the immediate reaction of Republicans to Johnson's program was, on the whole, deferential rather than critical. The task of restoring the Union, most Republicans agreed, was unprecedented, and involved problems that were too big and too troublesome for easy solutions.[7] Whatever views Republicans held privately went unspoken, for it seemed beyond dispute to many of them that Johnson's honesty was genuine, his efforts sincere, and his objects laudable. Moreover, the President had called his program "experimental," one subject to change both by conditions that might arise in the South, and by the review of Congress when it met later that year. For this reason, during the summer of 1865 no suggestion was ever made by the Republican leaders that Johnson's program was either inadequate or irresponsible, although they laid great emphasis on the experimental aspect of his program in the fall campaign of 1865.[8] This charge was made, but it came from the Democrats, who saw Johnson's program as an infringement on state rights and a dangerous exercise of executive power. Thus Washington McLean, Democratic boss of Hamilton County, was quoted in the *Cincinnati Daily Enquirer* for October 17, 1865, as saying: "We can't see it. Johnson's program is unconstitutional."

However, Republicans remained quiet only briefly, for by the end of 1865 the Republican attitude toward President Johnson's program had shifted to one of mild disappointment. There were several reasons for this significant development. First, as the President repeated his proposals for the South in interview after interview, it became obvious that his declared solutions, in his mind at least, were becoming less and less experimental and more and more final.[9] Second, with Johnson's express approval, the Republican press published a series of interviews which now made it clear that he had no program for the Negro, and that he would not brook debate about this "lapse" in his plans.[10] Furthermore, it became equally

clear that the President was anxious to have the South readmitted to the Union before a genuine debate on the problems
of reconstruction could begin, even if it meant—and it did—
accepting the old ex-Confederate leadership which was certain
to be elected under the terms of the North Carolina proclamation. The Republican leaders in Congress were not prepared
to engage in such a debate in company with former enemies
of the Union. They felt that these beaten foes should be allowed no part in such discussions, and for this reason Republicans began to talk about refusing admittance to the Southerners, even if they had been elected under the terms of the
President's North Carolina proclamation.[11]

The behavior of the Democratic party added to these
worries of the Republicans, for the Democrats began to shift
their support to the President. They now praised his program
as a model of statesmanship, hoping to see it carried through,
and hoping also to drive a wedge between Johnson and his
party. Democratic propaganda made much of the prospect of
a "Radical" conspiracy within the Republican party that
might overthrow Johnson and, at the same time, inflame
Northern passions against the South. The feelings of William
Dickson, a Cincinnati Republican, are typical of how the Republicans reacted to the Democratic strategy. On May 31,
1865, he wrote to Cox saying: "The Democracy have had private meetings here. I am this morning, in confidence, put in
possession of some of the results. . . . Their effort is to capture
President Johnson. . . . They expect aid from our divisions.
They hope the radicals will make war on Johnson on the question of negro suffrage: they will come to his support, hold out
to him expectations but finally treat him as they did Tyler.
This is the purpose of the enemy. To be forewarned is to be
forearmed." [12]

Republicans began to see the prospect that a new party
might be formed, composed of Johnson's most loyal supporters
and the Democrats. These suspicions arose in the context of
the wartime and postwar defections of Republicans to the
Democrats, and in the light of recent formations of third
parties at the local, if not at the national, level.[13]

In these circumstances it was natural for President Johnson to strike out upon a bold course of his own. He was a man who always kept himself informed of political developments in the localities. There, he saw that several Republican factions were abandoning their own party in order to join the Democrats or else that they were forming third parties with defecting Democrats. No one could deny that these new organizations were already coming into existence. For this reason, the President began to consult more and more frequently with the Democratic leaders in Washington, especially those from the South. Indeed, upon several occasions it seemed that he was striking up nothing less than a formal alliance with them.

Andrew Johnson realized at an early stage of the reconstruction era that he might be defied by his own party. Nevertheless, such was the nature of his belief in his own policy that he made early preparation to secure his own place as president even if it meant that he might forfeit the goodwill and allegiance of the Republicans who had carried him to office in the first place.

This general situation became even more complicated by the middle of the summer of 1865, when Republicans themselves began to use the issues of reconstruction for personal advantage, thus compounding an already chaotic situation.

The Ohio gubernatorial campaign of 1865 provides us with a good example of these factional quarrels in the Republican party. In that contest the Republican nominee for governor, Jacob D. Cox, was bitterly attacked by Samuel Plumb, the Republican mayor of Oberlin. The issue in dispute between the two men was that of Negro suffrage. They argued in spite of the fact that Republicans had decided to avoid any statement about Negro suffrage in the Republican platform in order to prevent bickering inside the party, which was not united upon that question.

Plumb, a candidate for the state legislature, publicly demanded that Cox should make clear his views upon the question. He wrote a letter to Cox on July 24, 1865, asking, in part: "We want to know directly from you your views on the following subjects: 1st. Are you in favor of modifying our Constitution so as to give the elective franchise to the colored men? 2nd. In the reorganization of the Southern states should the elective franchise be secured to the colored people?"

Plumb, anxious to embarrass Cox, cared little for the unity of the party, and he forced him to be explicit upon a subject that was certain to damage the general fabric of their cause. When Cox, under pressure of this kind, advocated a plan to colonize certain Southern states with Northern Negroes, the damage was done. (See Chapter Three.) Other Republican candidates announced their disagreement with this reactionary course, and certain Republican leaders tried to smooth over this whole matter, but their anger with both Plumb and Cox could not be concealed from the Democrats and from the public. With respect to Plumb's letter, for example, Aaron Perry wrote Cox on July 28, 1865: "An issue on present negro suffrage is a false issue. . . . Such an issue gives the reactionary elements every possible advantage. If the Oberlin or any other segment wants to fly the track, let it." As a result the unity of the party was dissolved during the heat of the campaign and the Republicans suffered at the polls in consequence.

A lack of party discipline of the same general kind also prevailed in the Cleveland area during this election. In Cleveland, in the eighteenth congressional district, trouble between the Republican leaders had manifested itself earlier in the year. It will be recalled that Edwin Cowles, the powerful postmaster of Cleveland, had been removed from his post by order of the President, who acted in this case upon the advice of Rufus Spalding, the congressman representing the Cleveland district. Cowles used his newspaper, the *Cleveland Leader* to strike back at the leaders of his own party and to support the cause of Negro suffrage in the South.

On July 3 and August 17, 1865, Cowles called upon Republicans in the eighteenth district to make Negro suffrage the leading cause in the fall campaign and to nominate for political office only those men who had pledged themselves to vote for the elimination of the word "white" from the franchise requirements in the Ohio constitution. Cowles was soon joined by a number of Republican ex-Democrats in other counties in the district. "Negro suffrage is the test," wrote the *Sandusky Register,* and again, on June 20, 1865, "We shall hold our Representatives and Senators to it." The *Cleveland Herald,* however, another Republican newspaper, followed the line adopted by the party upon the issue of Negro suffrage. "There is some grumbling about the platform," George Benedict declared, on June 24, 1865, in the *Cleveland Herald.* "Many think the question of Negro suffrage should not be dodged. We say dodged for dodged it was, and there is no use to deny the fact. The error the Convention made was a safe one. Better not go far enough than too far."

A spirited battle broke out between the two journals. The *Herald* accused the *Leader* of extremism and disruption. The *Leader* denounced its rival as the organ of compromise and opportunism. The Democrats in the district were delighted by the growing division among the Republicans over the issue of Negro suffrage. On August 21, 1865, the *Cleveland Plain Dealer* declared: "As the fight now stands, it is a most beautiful one, and proves that a family fight is always severe and bitter." As a result the Republicans in the Cleveland area lost all semblance of unity and, though they managed to retain the seat, their majority was much reduced.

The same dismal squabbling marred the performance of the Republican party in the nineteenth congressional district in Ohio. There, John Hutchins, a notorious cotton speculator, was anxious to secure the party's nomination for Congress in 1866. He spoke at the Republican State Convention in June, 1865, and again in August urging all Republicans in the district to speak out in favor of Negro suffrage. This was an attempt to embarrass James Garfield, the incumbent. Lyman Hall, editor of the *Portage County Democrat,* reacted by stating on July 11, 1865, that Hutchins was one of the most cunning and deceitful Republicans in the nineteenth district. During the Civil War, the *Democrat* charged: "Mr. Hutchins went to New Orleans as a sort of United States Treasury Agent. His position opened up for him a field of operations by which he is said to have grown suddenly, if not mysteriously, rich. . . . It is not pleasant to expose the moral obliquities and treacherous acts of this man as a politician. . . . It is due to the people that they should know the acts and style of this small-minded man, the leading elements of whose character are vanity, self-seeking, impudent assurance, unscrupulousness, mendacity and animosity."

Until this time Garfield had maintained a calculated silence, in conformity with the wishes of the party. Now, however, he was forced to announce grudgingly his support of a program of limited suffrage for the Negro in the South. On July 4, 1865, Garfield told his constituents: "In the extremity of our distress we called upon the black men to help us save the Republic. . . . we made a covenant with him sealed both with his blood and ours . . . that when the nation was redeemed he should be free and share with us its glories and blessings. . . . I am fully persuaded that some degree of intelligence and educational culture should be required as a qualification as a right of suffrage." (See the *Portage County Democrat*, July 12, 1865.) There can be no doubt that Garfield's private opinions upon the subject of Negro suffrage were quite different from his public pronouncements. On July 26, 1865, for example, Garfield wrote to Cox: "I confess to a strong feeling of repugnance when I think of the negro being made our political equal and I would be glad if they could be colonized, sent to heaven, or got rid of in any decent way. It would delight me." In consequence of these developments the Republicans were once again seen to be divided upon a subject of vital national importance.

Similarly, the senatorial contest in Ohio in 1865 witnessed an ugly dispute among Republicans. Senator John Sherman was challenged for his place by Robert Schenck, the congressman from the third congressional district, who wanted to become a senator.[14] In an attempt to gain adherents, Schenck pressed Sherman to declare himself upon the general issues of reconstruction, and he enlisted the support of the *Cincinnati Daily Gazette* in the campaign. In order to discredit the Senator the views of William Sherman, his brother, were given the widest publicity, for he was known for his intense hatred of the Negro, a reputation he acquired during the Civil War. It was said that his attitude toward the Negro amounted to "an almost criminal dislike." [15] Schenck and his allies sought to demonstrate that Sherman himself shared these sentiments.[16] After a difficult battle involving three roll calls Sherman was renominated, but the divisions in his party were plain for all to see.[17]

II

In 1867 the Congress of the United States passed a military reconstruction program for the South. Five military districts, each commanded by a major general, were established in the South.[18] The reaction of the *Cincinnati Daily Gazette* to the first Military Reconstruction Act of 1867 was typical of many Republican newspapers in Ohio. On February 19, 1867, the *Gazette* pointed out that Congress had finally put into legislation what "we say now, what we said in May, 1865, that the South must be garrisoned and kept under martial law. . . . The people don't want a theory of reconstruction. They want the substance." The *Gazette* also complained on April 24, 1867, that "two years, if not more, had been utterly lost by not conforming in 1865 to the simple fact that the Confederate States were conquered provinces under military government. . . . At any rate, time settles the issue." Charles Beard and Howard K. Beale have argued that military reconstruction was the result of a plot by Northern businessmen eager to keep the South out of the Union until they had fastened upon the country an economic system which would benefit their own class.[19] On the other hand, Eric McKitrick and John and LaWanda Cox blame President Andrew Johnson for the military solution to reconstruction. In their view Johnson blocked every suggestion of the Republican moderates for his own selfish purposes, until, as a result of their exasperation, they left the field to those Republican extremists who wished to impose only the harshest settlement upon the defeated South.[20] However, fresh examination of the condition of the Republican party at the local level in Ohio makes it clear that neither of those two interpretations is entirely valid.

The program of military reconstruction in the South did not result entirely from the machinations of businessmen in the North, nor did it occur only because of Andrew Johnson's quarrel with the mass of his party. The program of military reconstruction was the expedient hit upon by the new Republicans, men like Jacob Cox, James Garfield, and John Sherman, who wanted to preserve their party's national supremacy by keeping the South impotent as long as possible. They could not permit the South to reenter the Union with more political strength in Congress than it had enjoyed before the war began, a development which the abolition of the three-fifths ratio for representation made certain. Moreover, there was the possibility that, once in the Union, the South would form a political alliance with the Northern Democrats. These Republicans knew that such an alliance would drive their party from national power and thus achieve for the Democrats what they were almost powerless to bring about for themselves.

The Republicans needed to work out a scheme to prevent this from happening. One solution, which some Republicans advanced in the spring of 1865, was to confer the franchise upon Negroes in the South, for they expected that the Negro's vote would be cast for their party and thus furnish the basis for a measure of Republican political power in that region. However, many Republicans doubted that the federal government had the constitutional authority to dictate franchise requirements to a state. These Republicans proposed, instead, to reduce the representation in Congress of a state that denied the franchise to any of its adult male inhabitants. By means of this negative proposal the Republicans hoped to avoid granting suffrage to Negroes. Nevertheless, it was clear to them that, as long as the South remained under military supervision while Southerners worked at the required changes in franchise and representation, that region could not threaten the political supremacy of their party at the national level.

Nor were considerations of national power the only problem that dominated the thoughts of some Republicans. They wanted to create in Ohio a new Republican party along the most modern lines. Their object was to achieve that kind of unity and harmony which had eluded the Republican party for years past. The rapid return of the South to the Union would simply complicate their activities and make it more difficult for them. If they could reduce the South's political power, they could postpone a real threat to their party at the national level of politics. They would win time for themselves in the state during which they felt certain they could master their factious colleagues and produce a new Republican party organization capable of withstanding any challenge at the local level of politics.

Even though they were unable to achieve all their objectives, a significant part of the origins of the program of military supervision and reduced representation were brought about by their efforts.[21] For this reason, on June 23, 1865, one of the new Republicans, Robert Schenck, said in a speech in Columbus: "I hold that what we want is what can be a work of time. . . . I would not be in a hurry to bring them back this year or next year. . . . I don't care if [the South] . . . takes thirty years in coming back. . . . We should keep our hand upon them; have our military in charge of them. . . ." In the same way, on June 10, 1865, John Sherman declared in a speech at Circleville, Ohio: "I would leave them under military rule until they provide the only sure security for the future." On September 1, 1865, at Ravenna, Ohio, James Garfield said he would keep the South "on the mourner's bench for some time" by making certain that the military ruled over them. On September 2, 1865, Edward F. Noyes, later a governor of Ohio, said in a speech at Columbus that he advocated "the establishment of a . . . military force in each state to maintain order." [22]

In summary, these new Republicans were not like the extremists of their party who demanded the harshest solutions. The Republican extremists desired a complete social revolution in the South with far-reaching changes in the political leadership of the area, in land ownership, and in the suffrage.[23]

The new Republicans, however, were more concerned with the creation of a powerful national party. They believed that if the Southern states were readmitted to the Union, Southerners, in alliance with the Northern Democrats and dissident Republicans, would smash the Republican party, weakened by dissent, and thus come to control the destiny of the country.[24] However, if they could impose the program of military reconstruction to keep the South out of national politics for a sufficiently long period of time, the new Republicans felt that in the interval they could create a new, broad-based party that could defy any rival. Such a party would include those Democrats who were dissatisfied with the reactionary leadership and policies of their own party.[25]

The new Republicans were aware that national needs were not best served by their policy, that military control, as they envisioned it, merely postponed the resolution of some of the hard and gritty questions that would have to be resolved sooner or later. The program was a sheer makeshift and stopgap.

III

Along with the plan of military reconstruction the new Republicans also devised a solution to the important question of representation. This program was linked in their minds with their military proposals for the South as yet another method by which they could prevent an alliance between a powerful Southern faction and the Northern Democrats. (This question of representation commanded a great deal of public and congressional attention, for developments of great consequence were bound to follow from it.)

One method of apportioning representation to Congress was that of "total population." Under this method the population of each state in the Union would determine the number of its representatives in the Congress. However, Republicans objected to this plan of representation because the South would gain twelve additional seats in Congress as a result of Southern Negroes being counted in the total of the state. (As we have seen, in the period before the Civil War, Southern representation in Congress had been based on the whole number of white citizens and three-fifths of the Negro slave population.) It seemed intolerable to Republicans that the South, beaten in the war, should gain by the total population plan what it had been unable to achieve by force of arms. John Sherman's reaction to this possibility was typical of that expressed by most Republican leaders in Ohio. On June 10, 1865, he told his audience at a political rally: "Suppose you deny them [Negroes] suffrage, what then? The Southern States gain by the freedom of their slaves fourteen new members of Congress and as many electoral votes. Not three-fifths but five-fifths are counted. If you give the same men who revolted this increased political power, what safety have you? . . . We must have security for the future." [26]

A second method of apportioning representation to Congress was that of "legal voters." Under this method representation in Congress would be apportioned according to the number of people in each state who had the right to vote. Eastern Republicans objected to this plan because the enfranchised male populations in these states were smaller than they were in the Midwestern states and the easterners were bound to lose seats in Congress were the scheme adopted.[27]

The question of representation was hotly debated by Republicans in every part of the country. While this argument went on the new Republicans in Ohio, as a result of their local experience, had already hit upon a solution. This kind of "solution" to the question of Negro suffrage had been advocated by certain Republican leaders in Ohio since the end of the Civil War. On June 10, 1865, John Sherman, for example, declared: "I conclude, therefore, on the subject of negro voting, that in all the states that can claim their full rights under the Constitution, it is a question for the State, and that in revolted States, it is a question of policy and military government, to be decided by the national authorities. . . . In some of the Southern States I would leave them under military rule. . . ." [28] Furthermore, on June 21, 1865, Robert Schenck said in a speech in Cincinnati that there should be an amendment to the Constitution providing that "representation in Congress shall be in proportion to the voters, you have got an inducement to let all your people vote, no matter what their color. Then perhaps we will agree to admit you back. . . ." Richard Smith, editor of the *Cincinnati Gazette,* wrote in his paper on July 27, 1865: ". . . make representation in Congress proportional to the number of people allowed to vote. . . ." Edward Noyes, in a speech at Columbus on September 2, 1865, urged that the Constitution should be amended "to make representation dependent upon and proportional to the persons having a voice in such representation." Clark Waggoner wrote in the *Toledo Blade* for August 10, 1865: ". . . let the Constitution be amended basing the number of representatives on the actual number of voters in each state."

Their plan, which later became a significant part of the Fourteenth Amendment, satisfied nearly every faction of the party. By its terms representation to the Congress would be apportioned on the basis of total population. However, any state that denied the franchise to its adult male inhabitants would have its representation reduced proportionately by decision of the Congress.[29]

By this arrangement the South could be forced to grant suffrage to its Negroes or suffer the penalty of reduced representation. At the same time, the Republicans avoided committing their party to the vexed question of suffrage for Negroes. Moreover, the Eastern Republicans were satisfied because they would not lose out as a result of the arrangement.[30]

IV

Although there had been an agonizing search for some unifying answers through a long and bitter summer, these answers were arrived at quite suddenly, and received swift support from Republican leaders. This fact was freely voiced by Republican papers in 1867.

Despite the arguments of certain historians, most Republicans in Ohio, led by the new Republicans, were eager to impose the program of military reconstruction upon the Southern states. As we have said, they were eager to do so in order to gain for themselves that period of time they needed to build up an effective Republican party organization in their state and in the other states of the North as well. In June, 1866, Congress passed the Fourteenth Amendment, which incorporated the very arguments on representation brought forward by the new Republicans in Ohio in the previous year. Many Republicans assumed that this amendment represented those terms the South would have to accept to gain readmittance to the Union. However, some Republicans were not prepared to grant readmission, even if the South should decide to ratify the Fourteenth Amendment.

On this subject Eric McKitrick wrote that the "Republican commitment to the Fourteenth Amendment as the terms for readmission was about as strong as it could well have been at this time, given the party's unwillingness as a body, to go the length of a full, explicit, and categorical promise." As we shall see, the sentiment among Republican leaders in Ohio *was* "full and explicit," but not in favor of readmitting the South to the Union upon the basis of the Fourteenth Amendment.[31]

Rush R. Sloan, Postmaster of Columbus and President of the Republican State Convention, said in a speech at Columbus on June 20, 1866 that Republicans were not agreed on the conditions for the readmission of the South into the Union. They were only agreed that the "South shall present itself in an attitude of undoubted and indisputable loyalty such as will guarantee and preserve the national life." This speech was made within two weeks of the passage of the Fourteenth Amendment by the Congress. In the same way the *Cincinnati Gazette* for December 28, 1866, wrote of the Fourteenth Amendment that it pushed "the virtue of magnanimity to the extreme." Congress, the *Gazette* argued, should come forward with a plan of reconstruction "which it can execute without asking the consent of hostile bodies" which were "in law incompetent to assent or dissent." The article dismissed the amendment as an "embarrassment to the Republican party." On January 9, 1867, the *Mahoning Courier* in an editorial entitled "Shall the amendment be made a finality?" declared, "Congress is therefore admonished not to barter away the freedom and the right to protection of these people by pledging itself to admit southern Representatives upon the simple ratification of the Amendment."

The opinions of many Republican leaders in Ohio were no less insistent on this point. In August, 1866, Lyman Hall, editor of the *Portage County Democrat,* expressed a qualified approval of the Fourteenth Amendment because it enabled the Republican party to campaign in the congressional elections of that year with some kind of a reconstruction program. However, Hall made it clear that he was not prepared to jeopardize the safety of the country for the sake of a program that had no provision for the military occupation of the South. In the same way Samuel Shellabarger, congressman from the seventh congressional district, criticized the Fourteenth Amendment as the basis for the South's readmission to the Union. "This is clemency run mad," he told his constituents in Ohio. Rutherford B. Hayes, for his part, understood that the Fourteenth Amendment was simply one "condition" for the South to meet before it could be readmitted to the Union. As early as February, 1866, Hayes wrote to Murat Halstead:

> The South will never give up its power if admitted with it. I would be disposed, I think, to let in the loyal Tennesseans when their state adopts it. The rebel States will always be represented (during our day, at least) by Repudiators—men willing to assume every sort of claim payable South. Twenty-two Senators added to the twelve or fifteen now there, and the political power of four millions and a quarter negroes in the House and the Electoral College, is a serious thing.[32]

It seems possible that it was President Johnson's desire to secure the readmission of the Southern states as quickly as he could so that in the 1868 election their votes could help him hold his office. For this reason, if this possibility is a valid one, he was opposed to any plan of reconstruction that would delay the readmission of the South to the Union. (As we have said, many Republicans also were hostile to a policy of reconstruction, but it was their object to keep the Southern states out of national politics for as long as possible.) Later, after Republican programs and projects for the South had been agreed upon, party newspapers in Ohio argued that Johnson's "insane desire to be President" in 1868 was the most important factor in the political crises that had gripped the country for nearly three years.[33]

The Democrats, of course, were delighted to bring home to Johnson the unlikelihood of his receiving the nomination from Republicans and encouraged him to believe that he might find it with them if he broke with his party. With this ploy in mind Clement Vallandingham wrote to William Allen, a Democratic leader in Ohio: "We have the game in our own hands. Let us play it boldly and strongly." [34] The Republicans, for their part, warned the President to dismiss this appeal as the calculations of a party without political surprises of any kind. On March 22, 1866, for example, Cox wrote to President Johnson: "I am convinced that the leaders of the Democratic party are hypocritical in their support of the administration and your policy."

One way for Johnson to bring this break about was to foment a quarrel with Republicans and build bridges elsewhere. If he played his hand correctly, it might be possible to form a new political coalition which would align the Democrats with dissident Republicans. Such a coalition, combined with his supporters in the South, might carry him to the presidency again, and in his own right.

Republicans in Ohio called this coalition the "new party scheme." On January 27, 1866, Henry Boynton, Washington correspondent for the *Cincinnati Daily Gazette*, reported: "It has been hinted that a movement has been going on for weeks past to make a demonstration here, looking to the establishment of what in sugar-coated phrase is called a National party, the fact that it was to include Copperheads, Southern rebels, and a goodly proportion of neutrals being supposed to render it national."

V

When Congress reconvened in December, 1865, a joint committee was set up to initiate legislation on reconstruction. The work of this committee, called the Joint Committee of Fifteen, has been usefully discussed in detail by several historians. Their work, however, lacks information about those local developments which counted for so much at the time. The first result of the committee's labors was the extension of the Freedman's Bureau, which had been created in March, 1865. The committee now gave to this agency the power to protect the Negro against local violence and the deprivation of his civil rights. President Johnson promptly vetoed this bill. Few Republicans in Ohio remonstrated with him, for most were convinced that their worst suspicions were true: at best Johnson cared nothing for the party, and at worst, he would destroy it or watch it collapse under the weight of its own dissensions. However, John Russell, an ex-governor of Ohio, did react by writing his wife on February 22, 1866: "The vote seems to give great comfort to rebels, and their sympathizing Butternut friends." The Democrats, of course, were delighted with the President's veto.[35]

The President's veto was the result of calculation and circumstance. His chief object was to quarrel with the Republican party so that the Democrats and dissident Republican factions would rally to his personal standard. The Republicans struck back at him by passing the Freedman's Bureau Bill over his veto. At the same time they complained that his actions were determined by his rapacious desire to build a new party of his own, the "Presidential Party," as they contemptuously called it.[36] Again, in order to reaffirm their hostility to the President, the Republican Congress passed the Civil Rights Bill in March, 1866, and the Fourteenth Amendment in June of that year. For his part, the obstinate President proceeded to veto the Civil Rights Bill and to urge the Southern states not to ratify the Fourteenth Amendment. An aroused Congress passed them again despite his actions.

The stage was now set for the fall congressional elections of 1866. Prior to the campaign, President Johnson had called for the formation of a new party—the "National Union" party.[37] The support he had expected—support which the local situation in Ohio had promised as a possibility—was not forthcoming. Johnson's extremism, his unbending will, his cavalier attitude toward his party, and his lack of public support frightened Republicans away from his cause. As we mentioned above, Republicans were also angered by what they looked upon as his blatant self-seeking.[38] Nor, despite Johnson's hopes, did the Democrats join the new party. They were wary about forming a new party and abandoning their old organizational attachments.[39] It was now clear that the Democrats had used Johnson as he had hoped to use them. "Each was cheating the other," wrote the *Cincinnati Daily Gazette* on October 20, 1866.

In the face of these difficulties, Johnson was defeated. The Republicans, campaigning almost exclusively against his reconstruction policy, were completely victorious.

In order to understand the matter we must now pause in our analysis to examine the election results more closely. Eric McKitrick, in his *Andrew Johnson and Reconstruction*, remarks, in connection with the 1866 fall elections, upon "the sweeping character of the Republican victory." He also writes:

> In November, when all the Ohio returns were counted, the Republicans had carried the leading state offices by over 40,000 votes and had won seventeen out of nineteen congressional seats. Elsewhere in the North it was pretty much the same, in every state where a governorship was contested, it was the Republican who won it; every state legislature was carried by Republicans; and every Northern delegation to Congress was dominated by Republican majorities.[40]

So far as Ohio is concerned these statements are misleading, at least in part, and they reveal little genuine understanding of what was really taking place in the various congressional districts of the state.

The Republican majority of 40,000 votes, which McKitrick cites, is misleading because the official returns combined
the votes cast for the regular candidates of the Republican
party with those of the Republican dissidents who ran as
Independent candidates. The votes for the latter can hardly
be said to have been cast for the Republican party. The dissident Republicans usually cooperated with the Democrats
against the Republican party at the local level in Ohio, and in
most of the congressional districts of Ohio the Republican
majority was very seriously reduced, compared with 1864, as
a result of these alliances. Of even more significance is the fact
that this general reduction in Republican strength in 1866
foreshadowed the defeat of the party in the 1867 state elections, and the further reduction of their majorities in the 1868
congressional elections.

A glance at the table (pp. 64–65) reveals those significant
trends which have been partly ignored in the historical
literature. The figures reveal that in three out of Ohio's
nineteen congressional districts Republican majorities in 1866
were *very seriously reduced* from those they enjoyed in 1864.
There were *substantial reductions* in Republican majorities in
ten of the remaining sixteen congressional districts in 1866.
The Republicans increased their majority in 1866 in only one
congressional district, the seventeenth, an urban area encom-
passing Cleveland. The Republican party managers for these
Ohio districts could not be sanguine about their victory in the
elections, even though they were delighted at having won.

It might be argued in this connection that the reduction
of Republican majorities would occur as a matter of course in
the period after the Civil War. However, as our table shows,
the decline in Republican strength continued at an even
greater rate in the 1868 elections. The party, it is clear, was
affected by long-term trends which extended far beyond the
issues of the war.

Looked at in another way these figures show that in the 1866 election the Democrats won two seats, while in the 1868 election they won no less than six. Furthermore, in eight of the remaining thirteen districts in 1868 the vote was almost evenly divided between the two parties even though the Republican in each of these cases managed to win a meagre and unimpressive victory.

In addition to examining the figures produced by the electoral returns, it is also necessary to glance at what was taking place in the Ohio electoral districts in order to gain a clear picture of the Republican party at this time.

VI

The Republican party suffered a serious setback in the 1866 campaign in Ohio's first congressional district, represented in Congress by Benjamin Eggleston. He was a pugnacious ex-army officer who worked in close collaboration with Richard Smith, the editor of the *Cincinnati Daily Gazette*.[41]

Eggleston had good reason to worry in the months preceding the 1866 elections. Since his election to Congress in 1864 he had outraged a number of Republicans in the first district by his use of congressional patronage, and these men therefore organized themselves to bring about his defeat.[42] He also had cause for concern because the Workingmen's party was formed at this time, and it united men from both the major parties. The Workingmen's organization upset the politics of the district by applying pressure in both parties to protest against the condition of the urban worker. In the two years following the war, Independent candidates for local and state offices appeared in several elections, sometimes in support of the Workingmen, sometimes in opposition to the Eggleston faction of the Republican party. (See Chapter One.)

As a result of this situation, Eggleston's majority in 1866 was seriously reduced from 2429 votes in 1864 to 926 votes. Two years later, he again stood for reelection. On this occasion the opposition from within his party and the strength of

	VOTE IN CONGRESSIONAL DISTRICTS		VOTE IN STATE ELECTION	
	1864	*1866*	*1886*	*1867*
1.	*Republicans* 17,357 57%	*Republicans* 19,918 52%	*Democrats* 20,755 50.5%	*Republicans* 38,398 51.9%
2.	17,617 59%	20,540 56%	*Republicans* 22,891 51%	
3.	25,884 55%	28,987 51%	32,111 50.7%	*Democrats* 29,402 57%
4.	*Democrats* 21,676 56%	24,372 54%	*Democrats* 26,683 50.1%	*Republicans* 24,947 50.1%
5.	*Republicans* 20,005 52%	*Democrats* 24,396 55%	25,994 59%	*Democrats* 25,894 60%
6.	22,788 55%	*Republicans* 26,113 53%	*Republicans* 27,098 51%	26,060 55%
7.	22,343 57%	25,203 54%	27,851 50.1%	*Republicans* 25,778 50.5%
8.	19,886 54%	21,568 54%	23,448 52%	22,833 50.5%

#								
9.	25,228	53%	29,175	52%	*Democrats* 30,999	53%	*Democrats* 29,270	53%
10.	22,637	51%	27,828	53%	30,102	52%	27,549	51%
11.	*Democrats* 19,374	58%	22,728	56%	*Republicans* 25,134	52%	*Democrats* 24,067	52%
12.	24,314	52%	*Democrats* 25,882	46%	*Democrats* 27,661	58%	27,214	61%
13.	*Republicans* 23,527	50.4%	*Republicans* 26,168	50.5%	27,594	53%	26,906	54%
14.	23,156	55%	25,281	53%	*Republicans* 26,688	50.8%	*Republicans* 25,801	50.9%
15.	22,411	57%	23,568	54%	26,580	51.8%	*Democrats* 25,641	53%
16.	23,496	52%	25,316	52%	27,098	50.7%	25,867	50.4%
17.	21,504	59%	23,192	60%	*Republicans* 26,600	56%	*Republicans* 24,740	54%
18.	21,133	68%	22,453	64%	30,339	60%	26,628	60%
19.	24,401	74%	25,738	71%	29,946	67%	22,095	70%

the Democrats was too great for him to overcome. He was defeated in the congressional elections of 1868. For the first time in over a decade the Democrats now represented the first district in Congress.

The vote of the Republican party also declined in Ohio's second congressional district in the autumn elections of 1866. Rutherford B. Hayes, the Republican candidate for Congress, was reelected, but his majority was reduced from that he held in 1864. (He was opposed by Theodore Cook, a Democrat and ex-Republican who had the support of the Workingmen's organization, which held its greatest strength in this district.) The next year Hayes was elected governor of Ohio, and the Republicans of the second district nominated Richard Smith to replace him in Congress. The Democrats made no nomination. They voted instead to support Samuel Cary, who had been nominated by the Workingmen's party. Cary won the election against the official Republican. It was not merely a question of losing the election for Smith. He also realized that, by the terms of Cary's arrangements, all the immediate and solid benefits of the "Workingman's movement" lay upon the side of the Democrats. After his defeat Smith wrote in the *Cincinnati Daily Gazette* for October 9, 1867: "The people could not be blind to the fact that this dishonorable bolter from a Republican nomination which he had sought was in coalition with the managers of the Democratic party, and this while he was pretending to be a Republican, he was the candidate of the Democratic party, who were using him to destroy the Republican organization."

In 1868 Job Stevenson, the Republican candidate, was elected to Congress, but his majority was smaller than it had been for any Republican since the formation of the party in 1855. As in the case of the first congressional district, the splinter groups among the Republicans had seriously affected the fortunes of the party's official nominee.[43]

The pattern was the same in Ohio's third congressional district, represented by Robert Schenck. In 1866 Schenck sought reelection to Congress. He was opposed by Durbin

Ward, an ex-Republican who broke with his party in 1866 to become the nominee of the Democrats. Ward, and those Republicans who followed him out of this party, joined forces with the Workingmen's organization in the district. (See Chapter One.) He identified himself as an Independent Republican, even though he was supported by the Democratic party. As a result of this faction fight Schenck's majority was reduced in 1866. Two years later, Schenck's margin of victory was reduced even more drastically. W. D. Bickham, the editor of the *Dayton Journal,* explained the difficulties that Schenck faced in 1868 in the *Journal* for April 1, 1868, in the following way: "In wards where they [Democrats] feel strong enough to elect their partisans, they are independents; in those wards where they have no such chance, they are ready to coquette with anybody who will aid in humiliating the Republicans."

The incumbent Republican congressman in Ohio's fourth congressional district was William Lawrence. In 1866 Lawrence was opposed by John McKinney, an ex-Republican who had run as an Independent in 1865 and had been elected mayor of Miami.[44] In 1866 McKinney, although he still identified himself as an Independent Republican, was endorsed by the regular Democratic organization against Lawrence. As a result of this, Lawrence's majority in the fourth district was diminished after the election of 1866. An editorial in the *Miami Union* bears witness to the anger of Republicans in the fourth district over McKinney's course in 1866. On September 23, 1866, the *Miami Union* declared: "The copperheads are playing what they doubtless consider a shrewd game in this Congressional district. . . . McKinney was elected to Congress once by Union votes and basely betrayed those who so elected him. . . ."

Two years later, Lawrence was reelected to Congress only by the slender margin of 629 votes, for he was again opposed by Republican factions that refused their support to the official candidate of their party. He was not supported in part because Lawrence was opposed by William West, an ex-Republican, in 1868. West had sought the nomination of his party for Congress at the Republican district convention in August, 1868. Lawrence, however, was nominated for a third term and West and his allies bolted the convention. He then accepted the nomination from the Democratic party.[45]

The story was the same in Ohio's seventh congressional district, which included the city of Columbus. The incumbent Republican congressman, Samuel Shellabarger, had been elected to Congress by an overwhelming popular vote in 1864. Shellabarger was opposed, after the war, by an Independent party led by Thomas Miller. Miller had left the Republican party in 1865 in the hopes that President Johnson would confer upon him the power to distribute political offices in the seventh congressional district in order to pursuade other Republicans to join in a campaign against Shellabarger. This, however, did not happen.[46] Instead, Miller received support in 1865 for his Independent movement from the Democrats, and in the state elections of that year various Independent candidates appeared on the regular Democratic ticket for local and state offices. Shellabarger ran for reelection to Congress in 1866. He was opposed by Miller, who still identified himself as an Independent Republican. Shellabarger was reelected, but his margin of victory was less than it had been in 1864.[47] Shellabarger had been prepared to withdraw from an active course in Republican politics in 1866, in the face of serious opposition from within his party. He finally did refuse to stand for reelection in 1868. As a result, the Republican margin of victory was reduced to less than one-half percent of the total vote cast in the district.[48]

Republican James Ashley, the incumbent congressman in Ohio's tenth congressional district, was vitally concerned about the unity of his party, and with good reason. Two years earlier a coalition of Independent Republicans had joined forces with the Democrats of Toledo and came within 800 votes of defeating Ashley's bid for reelection to Congress. No Independent party was formed in 1866, but Ashley was plagued by factious Republicans who remained determined to put an end to his political career. Their conduct was a powerful influence in reducing his margin of victory in 1866 to less than 300 votes.

They finally defeated Ashley in his bid for reelection to Congress in 1868. (See Chapter One.)

No Republican was in more difficulty with his party than Columbus Delano, congressman from the thirteenth congressional district. From the earliest days of his election to Congress in 1864, Delano, an ex-Whig, faced bitter opposition from a faction of Republican ex-Democrats, who were critical of his moderation and compromises among the conflicting opinions of his colleagues in Congress.[49] These dissenting Republicans openly cooperated with the Democrats to reduce his majority in 1866 to one-half percent of the total vote. (In fact, George Morgan, the Democratic candidate, carried the district by 271 votes. However, Delano contested the voting returns in several areas in the district, and was finally awarded the election.) Two years later, in his third bid for reelection to Congress, Delano was refused renomination, due to opposition within his own party. The Republicans selected Charles Cooper, a newcomer to politics, instead. Even so, the Democrats went on to win the election, for the Republicans could not even unite behind their replacement for Delano.[50]

VII

For the most part the policies, attitudes, and practices of the Democrats were determined for them by their Republican opponents. For example, when the Republicans divided upon the issue of Negro suffrage, the Democrats blandly explained that they were opposed to suffrage of any kind for the Negroes. When the Republicans quarrelled over the terms required for the readmission of the South to the Union, the Democrats urged speedy readmission and a general leniency toward all ex-Confederates.[51] Furthermore, the Democrats seized upon whichever of these issues would cause most dissension in the Republican ranks in each congressional district. The question of Negro suffrage might serve them best in one district, the issue of reconstruction in another, the Republican connection with monopolists and bondholders in yet a third district. The Democrats regularly sought to extend those breaches and divisions which already existed in the Republican ranks by publicizing them.[52] A leading article in the *Cincinnati Daily Enquirer* for January 9, 1866, echoed the comments of the Democratic newspapers in the state: "Our contemporaries of the Republican party are losing their tempers. . . . They have lost their cohesive force by parting with the moral basis of their organizations. In fact, instead of being a united party the Republicans are divided into two or more discordant factions, hating each other worse than either of them hates the Democracy."

The Democrats also labored to widen the gaps that were now opening between President Johnson and his party. They remained uncommitted to the President, but they encouraged the talk of a coalition between the President's supporters and their own party. To further this end, the Democrats also sought to join to themselves those splinter groups of Republicans who were unable to agree with the official line urged upon them by their party.

It has been suggested that in the years immediately following the Civil War the Democrats concentrated almost exclusively upon the question of Negro suffrage in order to advance the fortunes of their party.[53] This, of course, was not quite the case, as our examination of political developments at the local level in Ohio has indicated. The Democrats, as a result of Republican dissensions, had numerous issues they could raise against their opponents. The Republicans, however, could offer no effective defense against these attacks, owing to the very nature of their party. The Republican party had been a loose amalgam since its origin in 1854. It was composed of all kinds of political groupings and factions that could coalesce effectively only upon rare occasions; this helps explain why the party remained less forceful than it might have been in the country during the decades following the Civil War.[54]

While it remained the party in power, the Republicans were required to solve the question of reconstruction. Men were becoming annoyed by the complexity of the debates upon the matter and the time they consumed. The American public wanted a solution to the problem and they wanted it within a

reasonable period of time.[55] While the Republicans were forced
to concentrate their energies upon reconstruction they opened
themselves to Democratic attacks concerning other issues which
had begun to assume more significance at exactly this time.
For example, workers were demanding an eight-hour day. The
condition of the cities and numerous other urban issues now
became themes of urgent importance. Financial policies and
questions concerned with taxation, always issues of moment
for an incumbent party, also demanded the kind of attention
the Republicans were unable to spare.[56] The Democrats were
able to gain genuine political advantages from each of these
issues.

The whole political scene was further complicated, for the
Republicans were forced to work out their programs under the
nominal leadership of a president who disagreed with them on
the most important problems of the day.

VIII

In February, 1867, Congress passed the First Military
Reconstruction Act, which must be understood if we are to
comprehend the relationship between policies at the local level
and national legislation dealing with reconstruction.[57]

The Act was written in two parts. The first part dealt
with military rule in the defeated South. By its terms the ten
Confederate states were divided into five Military Districts.
Each of these districts was placed under the control of a major
general who was responsible for the discipline of his troops
and the maintenance of law and order in the district.

A second part of the Act provided for the reorganization
of the state governments on the basis of Negro suffrage. Under
its terms elections for state constitutional conventions were to
be held. In these elections Negroes were qualified to vote, but
those whites who had supported the Confederacy were dis-
qualified from the franchise. These constitutional conventions
were empowered, by the terms of the law, to elect a state
legislature and a governor. When a legislature for the state
had been elected, it had the authority to ratify the Fourteenth

Amendment. The state could then be readmitted to the Union.

Several factions within the Republican party had argued bitterly for a number of differing solutions to the problems of reconstruction. They had been unable to agree upon the principal features, however—Negro suffrage in the South; the disqualification from the franchise of white Southerners; the nature and extent of military rule in the Southern states. Thus, the reaction to the Act in Ohio when it was finally passed was one of deep disappointment. The *Cincinnati Daily Gazette,* for example, wrote on June 27, 1867: "The measure has brought neither the supremacy of law, nor public or personal security, nor peace, nor does it promise to bring them. The more it advances the further it will plunge into anarchy." Republican politicians in Ohio saw at once that the Act left too many grave and weighty problems unsolved. How were the constitutional conventions in the states to be called into being? Who were to rank among the disfranchised in the Southern states? Who were to be branded as disloyal and deprived of their politicial rights for significant periods of time? Were Negroes to be eligible to hold office at the state level or at the local level?

Most Republican leaders in Ohio had desired straightforward military rule in the South, and for an indefinite period of time. Such a bold solution to the problem would have helped Republicans to avoid those very issues upon which the various factions of their party disagreed. As a result, the unity of the party in Ohio would be secured almost at once.

However, the 1867 Act was the result of the interplay of a number of conflicting forces in the political life of the time. In the first place President Johnson was concerned over his own position as a presidential candidate in 1868. He deliberately quarreled with his party, therefore, lest they force through the simple solution we have mentioned and achieve a party unity that could overwhelm him.[58] It would have been impossible for him to build up that coalition of his dreams, a Johnsonian party in the North allied to the Southern Democrats, which would make certain of his reelection to the presidency.

In the second place the Democrats were eager to throw up obstacles that would prevent a speedy readmission to the Union of the Southern states for their own partisan reasons. As long as the Southern states were debarred from readmission, the Democrats could be certain that the various local Republican factions would disagree with each other on the proper terms and requisites for such readmission. As a result, the American people would blame the Republicans for the failure to work out a reconstruction policy, and the party would suffer in consequence (to the advantage of the Democrats).[59] For this reason, the Democrats voted against all those measures in Congress that promised to put an end to the Republican search for a reconstruction policy.

In the third place, and most important of all for our purposes, the Republicans were angry with themselves, or more accurately, with those splinter groups within their party who used the issues of reconstruction for purposes of narrow partisan advantage at the local level. A leading editorial in the *Cincinnati Daily Gazette* for November 13, 1867, typical of many, declared: "Long majorities, long continued, breed in themselves the elements of dissolution. . . . In time it raises contests inside the party more fierce than that with the common enemy. It makes personal ambitions more prominent. . . . It is continually adding to a sorehead class, whose desire for place has not been gratified, or who are jealous of the prominent influences of others."

Jacob Cox described the Republican party truthfully when he confided to his friend Aaron Perry, the Cincinnati lawyer: "It is utterly impossible to detect any nucleus of opinion or policy. It is every man for himself." [60]

The result was the Military Reconstruction Act of 1867, a patchwork of various policies, which involved a certain ambiguity that was probably deliberate. This ambiguity resulted from that fact that the Act tried to satisfy as many groups of Republicans as possible.

The Republicans had brought forward an inefficient and ambiguous act that performed few services for the nation and fewer for the party. The public condemned their handiwork.

The passage of the Act, however, also forced the Republicans to realize that when they concerned themselves with the great problem of reconstruction, they had not pursued national objectives but had sought base, narrow, and petty advantages at the local level. Even worse, perhaps, the Republicans revealed their party to the American public as an inefficient, bitter, self-contradictory, disunited collection of ambitious politicians who deserved to forfeit the confidence of the electorate.

NOTES

1. See James R. Richardson, *A Compilation of the Messages and Papers of the Presidents*, VI (Washington, 1908), 312–16, 318–31.

2. Other exceptions to President Johnson's amnesty proclamation included those Southerners who possessed taxable property valued at $20,000 or more.

3. Benjamin Wade to Charles Sumner, July 29, 1865, *Wade mss.;* see also, Garfield to James Comly, December 12, 1865, *James Comly mss.,* Ohio Historical Society; Alphonso Taft to Thaddeus Stevens, December 28, 1865, *Thadeus Stevens mss.,* Library of Congress; John Sherman to William Sherman, August 29, 1865, *William Sherman mss.;* R. P. L. Baber to Johnson, July 4, 1865, *Johnson mss.; Cincinnati Daily Gazette,* June 19, 1865; *Coshocton Age,* September 8, 1865; *Dayton Journal,* June 23, 1865.

4. Jacob Cox to Sherman, January 27, 1866, *Sherman mss.;* Benjamin Fenn to Johnson, September 11, 1865, *Johnson mss.;* see also speech by Robert Schenck at Chillicothe, August 23, 1865, in *Summit County Beacon,* August 24, 1865.

5. A. Moos to Sherman, June 30, 1865, *Chase mss.;* George Hoadley to Smith, June 5, 1865, *Smith mss.;* see also *Dayton Journal,* June 29, 1865.

6. The two most prominent studies of this subject were written by Leon Litwack, *North of Slavery: The Negro in the Free States, 1790–1860* (Chicago, 1961), and V. Jacque Voegeli, *Free But Not Equal: The Midwest and the Negro During the Civil War* (Chicago, 1967).

7. James L. Bates to Edwin Stanton, June 11, 1865, *Edwin M. Stanton mss.,* Library of Congress. See also, R. P. L. Baber to Johnson, July 4, 1865, *Johnson mss.;* Cox to Garfield, July 19, 1865, *Garfield mss.;* William Dennison to Cox, July 19, 1865, *Cox mss.; Cincinnati Daily Commercial,* May 31, 1865; *Columbus State Journal,* August 11, 1865.

8. See, for example, a speech made by John Sherman at Circleville, June 10, 1865, in *Cincinnati Daily Gazette,* June 12, 1865.

9. *Cincinnati Daily Commercial,* September 18, 1865; *Columbus State Journal,* November 2, 1865.

10. *Portage County Democrat*, December 13, 1865; *Cincinnati Daily Commercial*, December 2, 1865.

11. *Dayton Journal*, November 7, 1865; *Summit County Beacon*, November 30, 1865; *Toledo Blade*, November 1, 1865.

12. See the editorials on this subject in the following Democratic newspapers: *The Marietta Times*, November 30, 1865; *The Crisis*, October 4, 1865; *Cleveland Plain Dealer*, December 1, 1865; *Portsmouth Times*, December 2, 1865; *Cincinnati Daily Enquirer*, December 7, 1865.

13. *Portage County Democrat*, January 31, 1866; *Dayton Journal*, January 18, 1866; *Cincinnati Daily Gazette*, January 27, 1866.

14. Joseph Geiger to Sherman, December 11, 1865, *Sherman mss.;* see also Charles Martoon to Strohm, August 14, 1865, *Strohm mss.; Cincinnati Daily Gazette*, September 6, 1865.

15. See Henry Halleck to William Sherman, December 24, 1864, *William Sherman mss.;* Samuel Plumb to Garfield, August 7, 1865, *Garfield mss.*

16. See Rush Sloan to Sherman, May 25, 1865, *Sherman mss.; Cincinnati Daily Gazette*, September 8, 1865.

17. For the details of Sherman's reelection to the Senate see C. Moulton to Sherman, January 18, 1866, *Sherman mss.;* Richard Smith to Garfield, January 14, 1866, *Garfield mss.; Columbus State Journal*, January 16, 1866.

18. See Commager, *op. cit.*, pp. 480, 488, 491.

19. See, for example, Howard K. Beale, *The Critical Year: A Study of Andrew Johnson and Reconstruction* (New York, 1958), pp. 1–13, 8–9; Charles and Mary Beard, *The Rise of American Civilization* (New York, 1956), pp. 52–121.

20. McKitrick, *op. cit.*, pp. 274–325, 448–85; see also John and La Wanda Cox, *Politics, Principle, and Prejudice: 1865–1866* (New York, 1963), pp. 195–232; for the most recent expression of this argument see W. R. Brock, *An American Crises: Congress and Reconstruction, 1865–1867* (London, 1963), Chap. II.

21. The "Beale" thesis has been challenged by Stanley Coben in his "Northeastern Business and Radical Reconstruction: A Re-Examination," *The Mississippi Valley Historical Review*, XLVI (1959), 67–90. Coben points out that, so far as the Republican party was concerned, there was no unity among the leadership in support of an economic program which would benefit the interests of big business. We must be clear that the "new Republicans" were not alone in advocating a plan of military reconstruction for the South. However, those Republicans did take the lead and supply the initiative in support of that program, at least in Ohio.

22. See speech by Robert Schenck, June 21, 1865, at Columbus, in *Cincinnati Daily Gazette*, June 23, 1865; speech by John Sherman at Circleville, June 10, 1865, in *Cincinnati Daily Gazette*, June 12, 1865; speech by James Garfield at Ravenna, July 4, 1865, in *Portage County Democrat*, July 12, 1865; speech by Edward Noyes at Columbus, September 1, 1865, in *Columbus State Journal*, September 2, 1865.

23. See, for example, the interview with James Ashley in *Cincinnati Daily Commercial*, June 12, 1865. Among other things, Ashley told

reporters that the Republican party intended "to crush any party or any man who stood up against the universal enfranchisement of the country."

24. See, for example, a speech by John Sherman at Circleville, June 10, 1865, in *Cincinnati Daily Gazette*, June 12, 1865.

25. For the attempt on the part of the new Republicans to bring those Democrats into a new political coalition see John Howard to Sherman, February 8, 1866, C. S. Hamilton to Sherman, February 9, 1866, *Sherman mss.*

26. See the *Cincinnati Daily Gazette*, June 12, 1865.

27. For a discussion of this aspect of the debate between Republicans on the subject of representation to Congress, see Joseph James, *The Framing of the Fourteenth Amendment* (Urbana, 1956), pp. 56–58.

28. See the *Cincinnati Daily Gazette*, June 12, 1865.

29. See Section 2 of the Fourteenth Amendment.

30. For the satisfaction of Republicans in Ohio with the Fourteenth Amendment see Warner Bateman to Sherman, April 29, 1866, *Sherman mss.;* E. B. Sadler to Bateman, April 29, 1866, *Bateman mss.;* Joseph Barett to Smith, July 18, 1866, *Smith mss.*

31. McKitrick, *op. cit.*, p. 452.

32. See speech by Rush Sloan at Columbus, June 20, 1865, in *Cincinnati Daily Gazette*, June 22, 1865; *Mahoning Courier*, January 9, 1866; *Portage County Democrat*, May 9, 1866; speech by Samuel Shellabarger at Columbus, August 21, 1866, in *Summit County Beacon*, September 13, 1866; Hayes to Murat Halstead, February 2, 1866; *Hayes mss.;* see also *Columbus State Journal*, November 20, 1866.

33. See, for example, *Cincinnati Daily Gazette*, October 13, 1867.

34. Clement Vallandigham to William Allen, May 14, 1866, *William Allen mss.*, Library of Congress.

35. *John Russell mss.*, Ohio Historical Society. See also A. B. Buttles to Johnson, February 20, 1866, *Johnson mss.;* Alexander Long to Trimble, February 22, 1866, *Trimble mss.; Cincinnati Daily Enquirer*, February 21, 1866.

36. James Garfield to George Chaffee, March 24, 1866, *George Chaffee mss.*, Western Reserve Historical Society.

37. See the call for this convention in *Toledo Blade*, May 28, 1866; *Dayton Journal*, July 4, 1866.

38. For a discussion of the failure of the National Union Party see McKitrick, *op. cit.*, pp. 410–20. For the "unity" of the Republican party in Ohio in 1866 see William Ritezal to Garfield, May 31, 1866, *Garfield mss.*

39. M. Mitchell to William Allen, August 8, 1866, *Allen mss.*

40. McKitrick, *op. cit.*, p. 447.

41. For the details of the alliance between Eggleston and the "*Gazette* clique" see Robert Smith to Sherman, January 20, 1866, *Sherman mss.;* Robert Smith to Bateman, February 23, 1866, *Bateman mss.*

42. Bateman to Sherman, January 16, 1866, *Sherman mss.*

43. For Republican factionalism in the second district in 1868 see *Cincinnati Daily Gazette*, June 9, 1868, September 5, 9, 1865.

44. For a discussion of the "Independent movement" in the fourth district in 1865 see *Miami Union*, August 22, 1865.

45. See *Miami Union*, October 28, 1868. For a discussion of the alliance between the Democrats and the Independent Republicans in the fourth district in 1868 see *Miami Union*, March 28, April 4, June 13, 1868.

46. See Thomas Miller to Johnson, January 30, 1867, *Johnson mss.;* see also Amos Layman to Johnson, November 13, 1866, *Johnson mss.*

47. See *Portage County Democrat*, August 14, 1866.

48. See table, pp. 64–65; see also Shellabarger to Comly, May 18, 1866, C. M. Nichols to Comly, July 9, 1868, *Comly mss.*

49. A. Denny to Sherman, February 23, 1866, *Sherman mss.;* Warner Bateman to Smith, September 23, 1866, *Smith mss.; Cleveland Plain Dealer*, March 27, 1866.

50. See *Coshocton Age*, September 15, October 15, 1868.

51. *Cleveland Plain Dealer*, July 6, 1865.

52. For a discussion of the various aspects of the Democratic opposition in 1865 see McKitrick, *op. cit.*, pp. 67–76.

53. McKitrick, *op. cit.*, pp. 5f.

54. See Carl Degler, "American Political Parties and the Rise of the City: An Interpretation," *Journal of American History*, LI (1964), 41–43.

55. See, in this connection, the editorials in the *Portage County Democrat*, May 9, 1866; *Coshocton Age*, June 1, 1866. See also *Toledo Blade*, June 13, 1866; L. W. Hall to Garfield, April 12, 1866, *Garfield mss.;* E. B. Sadler to Bateman, April 29, 1866, *Bateman mss.*

56. Warner Bateman to Sherman, April 10, 1866; James Hall to Sherman, October 31, 1867, *Sherman mss.;* Smith to Robert Mussey, October 21, 1867, *Smith mss.*

57. See Commager, *op. cit.*, p. 480.

58. *Cincinnati Daily Gazette*, October 12, 1867; *Steubenville Weekly Herald*, March 8, 1867; *Miami Union*, January 2, 1867.

59. For a discussion of this aspect of the Democratic strategy in the controversy between President Johnson and his party over the issue of reconstruction, see McKitrick, *op. cit.*, pp. 460–67.

60. Cox to Aaron Perry, January 25, 1867, *Cox mss.*

The Black Hobby

CHAPTER THREE

I

Negro suffrage turned out to be the most terrible problem to confront the Republican party in Ohio following the Civil War. It proved to be so difficult for Republicans that within two years of the Union victory the Democrats in Ohio captured control of the state legislature and sent their candidate to the United States Senate in the place of the Republican incumbent. (Of course, there were other problems that contributed in varying measure to the Republican defeat of 1867.)

How did the issue of Negro suffrage come to exercise such a large and fateful influence upon the fortunes of the Republican party in Ohio? In order to answer this question we must first examine, however briefly, the relationship between the issue of Negro suffrage and reconstruction of the South. Republican leaders in Ohio realized that their party faced a difficult and dangerous situation in the task of reconstructing the South. The question of who should govern the South was clear enough, but the problem of defining the Negro's status in the reconstructed South was infinitely more complicated. What rights, for example, would Negroes now enjoy as free men? In the opinion of most Republican leaders serious and basic changes in the status of the Negro were required before the South could be readmitted to the Union.[1]

At the same time these leaders were well aware that racial prejudice was a distinguishing characteristic of their society. They knew that any attempt they made to confer more rights upon the Negro than most whites were willing to grant was certain to provoke considerable resistance, and expose their party to a crushing political defeat. As one Republican leader put it: "Color as a basis of suffrage is absurd, but a party in Ohio [that] would now commit itself to Negro suffrage would inevitably be defeated."[2] James Comly, editor of the influential *Columbus State Journal,* summed up the situation concisely in the *Journal* on September 11, 1867, with a comment that expressed the general feelings of most Republicans in Ohio. The Republican party, Comly wrote, has emerged from the war with a "colored elephant" on its hands.

There was yet another aspect of this question that deeply troubled some Republican leaders in Ohio. The party had been divided for many years into bitterly opposed factions, as we have seen. This had changed only in the period from 1861 to 1865 when the desperate events of civil conflict had forced Republicans to submerge their differences in the interests of the war effort. Now that the war was over, Republican leaders like Jacob Cox perceived the great danger that Negro suffrage was the kind of issue dissident Republicans might use to resume their factional quarreling. In June, 1865, Cox explained this fear to Aaron F. Perry, a close political friend. "The Negro suffrage question is in itself grave enough," Cox wrote, "but it is likely to be complicated by the ambition of politicians to make it a leverage on one side or the other."[3] And the Negro suffrage issue did come to serve this purpose.

II

In 1865 there were 40,000 Negroes living in Ohio, a larger number than had lived there before the war, yet it was only 1 percent of the whole population.[4] The distribution of these Negroes in the state was highly uneven. Over two-thirds of them were located in the southern half of the state; almost 8000 lived in Cincinnati. The largest increases in the Negro population since 1830 were in the cities, particularly in Cincinnati, Cleveland, and Toledo. For example, 1304 Negroes lived in Cincinnati in 1830. The number increased to 7432 in 1870.[5]

After 1802 regulations to prevent more Negroes from coming into the state were demanded with ever-growing frequency. In 1804 and 1807 the Ohio legislature passed the Black Laws. These laws compelled Negroes to post a $500 bond guaranteeing good behavior when they entered the state and to produce a court certificate as evidence of their freedom.[6]

In 1849 the antislavery reformers in the state won a significant victory when the Black Laws were repealed. Nevertheless, the victory only served to intensify the passion which raged round the Negro question. Many whites in Ohio were desperately afraid that large numbers of Negroes might migrate into the state from the South. These feelings account for the powerful reaction of Ohio's white residents to the Emancipation Proclamation. (See Chapter One.) Hostility to the proclamation was so strong that it often led to mob violence—especially among urban workers who looked upon the competition of the Negro as a threat to their own bargaining positions in the labor market. In Cincinnati, for example, raging mobs of white workers besieged the Negro community, burned homes, and forced some Negroes to find safety outside the state.[7] The reaction to Negro immigration at first was confined largely to those counties in Ohio that bordered on the Southern states. It spread throughout the state in the postwar period, and the Democrats were quick to exploit the dislike of Negro immigration for their own political advantage.

Many Republican leaders in Ohio, in the middle of 1865, were thus deeply worried about the task of reconstructing the Union and by the fact that no reconstruction program for the South could be devised without discussing the status of the newly freed Negro.[8]

III

Jacob Cox, a vigilant Republican leader, was the party's nominee for the office of governor. He was more concerned than many about the effects of the Negro issue upon the fortunes of the Republican party, and he saw his fears confirmed at the Republican State Convention held in the summer of 1865. Edwin Cowles, the shrewd and powerful editor of the *Cleveland Leader,* used his editorials to inject the issue of Negro suffrage into the arena of Republican politics. He urged Republicans to adopt a policy in support of the issue. On June 22, 1865, for example, Cowles defended his stand, declaring that the Republican platform was "chiefly remarkable for what it omits to say, than for what it says. It weakly and timidly ignored the only vital issue of the day—the great issue of negro suffrage. Besides this there is no other live issue on which parties are divided." In addition, Cowles advanced the extreme proposal that only those Republicans who accepted this policy should be nominated by their party for seats in the state legislature. In effect, Cowles made Negro suffrage the high "test" of party loyalty.[9]

Cowles' proposals were the result of a deep design. He and his friends, the Republican ex-Democrats in the party, realized even before the war was over that they were beginning to lose their influence in the councils of the party. They were planning to create a new party coalition composed of their own Republican ex-Democrat followers, and any others in the ranks of the party who might be induced to join their movement, in order to reassert their authority. (See Chapter One.)

Nor did Cowles confine his expectations to dissident Republicans. There was reason for him to hope that he could attract a significant number of Democrats to the support of his new organization as well. Contrary to accepted opinion, the Democratic party in Ohio was not united upon the issue of Negro suffrage. The strongest opposition to Negro suffrage came from Washington McLean, the leader of the Democratic party in southern Ohio. Along these lines, the *Cincinnati Daily Commercial* for June 16, 1865, argued: "The negro never asked for political rights, never wanted them, never deemed himself fit for them. . . . Therefore, the negro is destined to stay where he is, at all events, to stop going forward." However, many Democrats in the northern part of the state disagreed with his Negro policy. These Democrats supported some form of limited or "impartial" suffrage, as it was called by contemporaries, for Negroes in the South. They did so, not because they were sympathetic with the Negro in his plight, but because of their resentment of McLean, who was attempting to dominate the entire Democratic party from his stronghold in the southern area of the state. This "moderate" Democratic position upon the issue of Negro suffrage was expressed by George Pendleton, a prominent leader of that party in Ohio. On January 7, 1866, Pendleton wrote a letter to Nathaniel Pendleton of Virginia on the subject of Negro rights. This letter was widely published in newspapers throughout Ohio. In it, Pendleton argued: "Justice and good policy require that the negro be protected in his civil rights. . . . Sober second thought should persuade the South to take account of the exigencies of the times and forget prejudice." (This was published in the *Cleveland Plain Dealer,* January 19, 1866.) As a result of this split among the Democrats Cowles and his followers began to hope that they might be able to persuade some Democrats in the North to join them in the formation of a new party in the state. For months past, certain Republican ex-Democrats in Ohio *had* acted with high officials in the Democratic party to establish this coalition. (See Chapter One.)

In these activities Cowles, a master of politics and intrigue, was trying to gain an end of great importance. He wanted to support Salmon P. Chase of Ohio, Secretary of the

Treasury in Johnson's administration, as candidate for president in 1868. (See Chapter Five.) However, no organization
existed in the state of Ohio that could turn these plans into
hard reality, for the Republican party and its policies in Ohio
in 1865 were controlled by the ex-Whigs. They began to dominate the party in the mid-1850s. At that time the ex-Whigs
resolved, as one correspondent put it, to replace the ex-Democratic leaders of the Republican party with the "better elements" and their "invincible Whig prejudices." [10] They were
Chase's bitter enemies and had defeated his bids for the presidential nomination in both 1860 and 1864.

Chase relied upon the ex-Democratic wing of the Republican party, but this faction had been almost completely dis-
persed by the ex-Whigs. Edwin Cowles tried to gain their
support in an organized manner by demanding that all Republican candidates for the state legislature declare themselves in
favor of Negro suffrage. He realized the ex-Whigs would
oppose the idea, but he also knew that the ex-Democrats had
always supported measures designed to ameliorate the condition of Negroes. [11]

Chase's enemies in the Republican party realized Cowles'
intentions at once, and they proceeded to attack Chase in clear
and harsh words. The *Portage County Democrat* on July 4,
1865, for example, stated: "We feel sorry for Mr. Chase. . . .
On most subjects, he is sane—on the matter of the Presidency
he is not sound. . . . Chase is too ambitious and should realize
this fact."

Chase found the organized body of supporters in the state,
which had escaped him until this time. We should be clear,
however, that the ex-Democrats had confined their concern for
the Negro to the abolition of slavery during the prewar period.
They were either hostile or indifferent to the prospect of the
Negro's gaining political or social equality. Furthermore, the
ex-Whigs came to realize that if they became too warm in
their opposition to Chase, Cowles and his friends might create
a new party based upon the alignments we mentioned above.

A majority of Republicans on the Resolutions Committee

at the State Convention in 1867 refused to countenance Cowles'
suggestions because they were aware of the motives that lay
behind them, even if they did not know the details of the plan.
The Army delegates were strongest in opposition to Cowles. It
was completely unacceptable to them that Negroes should be
allowed to vote in Ohio.[12] They were so angered that they
threatened to bolt the convention and to campaign against the
party in the fall elections if Cowles' proposals were accepted.

An editorial in the *Cincinnati Daily Commercial* for June
23, 1865, summed up the conduct of the military delegates in
the following words: "There were no words wasted by the
army delegates . . . the soldiers are not in favor of reconstructing the Southern states on the basis of negro suffrage. . . . The
army delegates were quite peremptory, and it is even complained they were a little rough. . . ." [13]

George Wright, the President of the Resolutions Committee at the convention, strove desperately for some measure of
party unity in the face of those conflicting groups. Finally, his
committee passed a resolution, later adopted by the convention,
which declared that the Republican party supported the
principles set forth in the Declaration of Independence. This
action led many Republican newspapers in the state to de-
nounce the platform of their party in the severest terms. In
the words of the *Portage County Democrat* on June 28, 1865:
"It enunciates no vital living principle—unless perchance the
foggy reference to the Declaration of Independence, may be
regarded as such." John Sherman, the junior Senator from
Ohio, remarked: "The resolution is one of those glittering gen-
eralities that I like to see from time to time." [14]

Jacob Cox, however, could not derive the same kind of
satisfaction from the resolution, for he realized that Cowles
and his friends were less concerned with the fate of the Negro
in Ohio than they were with advancing their own narrow political objects. Actually, they sought to break up the unity of the
Republican party in order to dominate some of its factions
while they joined with the Democrats to form an entirely new
political party in the state.[15] Cox felt that the issue of Negro

suffrage Cowles had raised in Ohio was a "false issue," and he proposed to expose the true designs of Cowles and his friends by speaking out on the matter in public.[16]

Before Cox could act, however, Cowles and his friends decided to press him to declare himself upon the issue of Negro suffrage. One of Cowles' friends, Samuel Plumb, the mayor of Oberlin, wrote to Cox on July 28, 1865, in order to demand that he, as the party's gubernatorial candidate, adopt one position or another upon the question of Negro suffrage. (See Chapter Two.) Cox realized at once that Plumb's object was to disrupt the party further by injecting the very issue upon which he and his friends had been beaten at the June convention. In his reply to Plumb's letter, published in the *Coshocton Age* on August 11, 1865, Cox declared:

> Political organizations, like every other, are founded upon a mutual waiving of some articles of personal belief for the sake of securing united and effective action upon others. . . . and the bond of union can hardly be said to be kept in good faith when individuals of a party propound as tests to a candidate questions which were not acted upon by the convention, especially when such questions were notoriously excluded from the list of those upon which community of belief was demanded.

Cox also heard from Aaron F. Perry on the very day that he received Plumb's letter. (Perry was a prominent Cincinnati lawyer who represented another faction of the Republican party than that from which Plumb spoke.) Perry indicated that he agreed with Cox that their task was to defy Plumb and his friends, for the sake of the party. Buoyed up by Perry's support, General Cox decided to strike out in the strongest terms.[17]

On August 1, 1865, he wrote to Plumb and saw to it that his letter was released to the press within the week.[18] He adduced three general points that seemed to him significant in connection with the Negro issue. The General's first point explained that Negroes and whites could never live together in genuine harmony because of the racial prejudice of the white population. It followed, as his second point made clear, that any scheme which had as its purpose an attempt to create equality between the races was bound to fail. Cox's third point revealed how deeply he had been stung by the intrigues of the Cowles-Plumb faction of the party. Even though he realized that they were less concerned with the fate of the Negro than with the fortunes of their own political friends in the state, he struck out at the Negro in savage terms. He declared that in his opinion the key to the future of the Negro race in the United States lay not in the franchise but in "colonization." He proposed the extreme solution that four states—South Carolina, Florida, Alabama, and Georgia—be set aside for the Negro people. All the whites would be removed from these states and they would be "colonized" by Negroes, under the direction of the Federal Government.

Cox also condemned the Republicans who took advantage of the Negro issue, and their activities. He made it known that he was aware of their "guerrilla warfare" and hoped that they would now join the ranks of the "heavy column" of the majority, despite the agitation they had caused the party by their activities. It is important for us to notice that Cox hit upon this plan not as a result of vindictive feelings toward the South, not as a result of his concern for Negroes, but solely because he meant to defy those local politicians in Ohio who proposed to use the Negro issue to further their own particular designs in the political life of the state.

IV

The Republican party in Ohio reeled under the explosive effect of these pronouncements. For example, on August 2, 1865, William Sherman wrote to John Sherman that Cox's letter fell like a "bombshell" in the Republican camp. A political friend of Salmon P. Chase, Flamen Ball, was shocked by Cox's letter and told the Chief Justice: "Politics are wild in Ohio. Cox, your old friend, seems to have fallen into the arms of the conservatives and to have ignored all the former teachings of Oberlin."

Most Republican leaders in the state still looked back to the convention solution, to the bland statement that had committed the party to nothing at all save the principles of the Declaration of Independence. Now, however, every faction-monger in the state who desired to launch a breakaway movement of his own was presented with a golden opportunity. (See Chapter Two.) In this connection, Murat Halstead warned his party in the *Cincinnati Daily Commercial* on August 16, 1865: "If we suffer ourselves to be divided, we shall find our opponents united, and ready to take advantage of our weakness. Unity and harmony must, therefore, be our watchwords. . . . We cannot afford to let our differences of opinion separate us." In spite of the warning, Congressman Robert Schenck of Dayton decided to try to take John Sherman's seat in the United States Senate. Schenck and his followers therefore sought to condemn Sherman as an advocate of Cox's plan for Negro "colonization." [19] Sherman struck back by accusing Edwin Stanton, the Secretary of War in Johnson's cabinet and a friend of Schenck's, of using the resources of his department in order to meddle in Ohio politics, to Schenck's advantage.[20]

John Hutchins had similar intentions. He had never been concerned with the fate of Negroes in earlier years. In fact, he exploited Negro labor during the war. Nevertheless, he attacked James Garfield as one who was unconcerned with Negro rights. Hutchins began this campaign against Garfield in 1865 in order to seize his place as the Republican nominee for the nineteenth congressional district in Ohio in 1866.[21] Garfield, trying to avoid a squabble, maintained a dignified silence under these assaults even though he was distressed by the charge, and he managed to win the nomination.[22] (See Chapter Two.)

As yet a third example, Richard Smith, editor of the *Cincinnati Gazette,* urged that it was the duty of the Republican party to secure equal rights for the Negro in the South. He stated in his paper on June 15, 1865, that justice to the Negro required "that they who are called upon to bear arms and shed their blood in their country's defense should have all the rights of citizenship. . . ." This policy was stoutly opposed by Murat Halstead in his journal, the *Cincinnati Daily Commercial*. He was indifferent to the fate of the Negro and resisted Smith's arguments fiercely in the editorial columns of his paper. (See the editorials for July 31 and October 16, 1865.) In reality, Halstead and Smith were battling for the control of Cincinnati, the second congressional district of the state, and they chose to use the Negro question as the apparent issue.

Some Ohio Republicans, however, were genuinely in favor of advancing the cause of Negro rights. Flamen Ball, for example, a Cincinnati lawyer of some political influence, was passionately attached to the movement for Negro suffrage as a matter of principle and justice. "Negro suffrage," Ball wrote, "should be the crowning event" of the movement for Negro freedom. Republicans like Ball, moreover, were confident that many of their fellow citizens in Ohio were prepared to support them in this attitude at the polls.

Still other Republican factions in Ohio reacted in a somewhat different way when the issue of reconstruction and the Negro question were brought forward. Each of these groups was mainly interested in some other issue, and each was wearied to see its goals set aside because of the concern in the party about Negroes (which also annoyed them, for they knew it was a false issue as well). Some politicians in Ohio believed that social conditions and urban problems were more relevant in the postwar era than was the Negro question. Others stressed the importance of a protective tariff, of fiscal reforms, of changes in the banking laws, or economic legislation that might be more vital for the future well-being of the state and the nation than the fate of Negroes. Most of these Republicans felt that a military solution was necessary to the problem of reconstruction.

V

The Democratic leaders in Ohio were delighted to observe the bickering among Republicans over the Negro issue. In particular, Washington McLean, the Democratic leader in southern Ohio, felt that this question might help him to regain some of the authority he had lost in his party in recent years. McLean felt that opposition to Negro suffrage also was certain to win votes and adherents for the Democrats. More important, he saw that the Republicans could not unite even to oppose him on this issue. He therefore led the Democratic opposition to any plan that advocated suffrage for the Negroes. For this reason, in part, the Democrats made the issue of Negro suffrage the central issue of the campaign against the Republicans.[23]

George Morgan was the Democratic candidate for governor and a friend of McLean's. In a speech given at Elyria on September 12, 1865, and quoted in the *Cleveland Plain Dealer* two days later, he accordingly denounced the Republicans as the "party of the black man." He warned that if Republican policies were followed, the result would be a serious influx of Negro immigrants to the state of Ohio. He also raised the spectre of school integration. He charged again and again that Republican policies would lead to integrated schools in Ohio. In a leading article entitled, "Are you in favor of Admitting Colored Children into our Public Schools?" the *Marietta Times* declared: "If you are in favor of throwing open our public schools alike to the reception of colored and white children, vote for General Cox and the candidate on the same ticket with him."

The congressional campaign of 1866 turned upon the issue of the Fourteenth Amendment, an issue that encompassed practically all the arguments both parties had raised about the Negro in the previous year. On the one hand the Republicans constantly maintained that the Fourteenth Amendment merely served to protect the Negro in his life, liberty, and property. As Richard Smith, one of their leaders and editor of the *Cincinnati Gazette,* wrote in September: "The Fourteenth Amendment has nothing whatsoever to do with the franchise." [24] On the other hand, the Democrats held that the Amendment gave the franchise to the Negroes. They added that such a development would lead inevitably to the integration of the public schools in the state.[25] These arguments proved to be so telling and effective that the Republicans, in order to maintain themselves at the polls, found it necessary to come forward as a white supremacy party—a party that promised the public to be ever vigilant in defense of the position of the white population in Ohio even though they occasionally gave some lip-service to the Negro cause.[26]

The results of the election had a sobering effect on the Republicans. They won the election, but their majorities were seriously reduced. (See Chapter Two.) The Republicans could see that the issue of Negro rights, and in particular the issue of granting the franchise to the Negro, had very seriously damaged their party at the polls—that their party had been weakened as a result of its perennial faction fights. The Republicans were forced to realize that the Democrats were now in a much better position to face the political future in the state of Ohio. The Democratic party did not suffer so severely from factional rivalries. Moreover, the Democrats were able to draw upon solid blocs of voters composed of the immigrants and the urban workers who were staunchly loyal to the party.

The Republicans, in their distress, tried to make a virtue of their disunity. Republican newspaper editors began to stress a certain pride in the tolerance of individual opinion that marked their party while they condemned the Democrats as a party that voted slavishly for its candidates simply because they were Democrats, regardless of beliefs, views, and principles.[27]

VI

By the beginning of 1867 some Republican leaders saw that they were confronted by two serious problems: the regular and "machine-like" adherents of the Democrats—the urban workers and immigrants—could be relied upon to vote against any and all Republican candidates; the Republicans would lose the support of many white men in Ohio if the party continued to advocate the vote for Negroes. As one of them put it, the first task of their party was "to get the nigger out of politics." [28]

The Republicans, however, could look upon enfranchised Negroes as adherents who would be as loyal to their party as the urban workers and immigrants were to the Democrats. There were approximately 10,000 Negro men in Ohio who could be regarded as Republican voters if the law gave them the franchise.[29] Their votes could be decisive in deciding elections, especially in the so-called doubtful counties in the central part of the state, where the margin between the two parties was very small. For example, the Republican majority in Muskingum County in 1865 had been a mere 60 votes, but there were 400 Negro males of voting age living there who could have increased that majority. In Ross County the Democrats had won the election of 1865 with a majority of 103 votes; more than 460 male Negroes of voting age lived in the county. They could, perhaps, have helped the Republicans win.

The Columbus State Journal on September 11, 1865, published a complete list of those counties in Ohio in which the vote of the Negro would mean the difference between victory or defeat for the Republican party. The newspaper commented: "This may be regarded as a selfish appeal to our friends in behalf of the amendment, but it is such an appeal that may well reach many men on whom any argument as to the abstract justice of manhood suffrage would be lost."

The Republican leaders in Ohio tried to overcome the problems in the interest of narrow party advantage. This conclusion conflicts with the arguments of a number of historians. La Wanda and John Cox have written, for example, as follows:

> In challenge to the dominant pattern of interpretation . . . we should like to suggest that Republican party leadership played a crucial role in committing this nation to equal suffrage for the Negro not because of

political expediency but *despite* political risk. Race
prejudice was so strong in the North that the issue of
equal Negro suffrage constituted a clear and present
danger to the Republicans. . . . The exploitation of
prejudice by the Democratic opposition was blatant and
unashamed. . . .

In Ohio the issue was clearly drawn, for, in addition to the nationwide commitment to Negro suffrage
in the South made by the First Reconstruction Act of
March, 1867, the Republican party bore responsibility
for the state-wide referendum on behalf of equal suffrage at home. . . .

In short, Republican sponsorship of Negro suffrage
meant flirtation with political disaster in the North,
particularly in any one or all of the seven pivotal states.
. . . Included among them were the four most populous
states in the nation. . . . New York, Pennsylvania, Ohio,
and Illinois. . . . If Negroes were to be equally enfranchised . . . it is true that Republicans could count upon
support from an overwhelming majority of the new
voters. It does not necessarily follow, however, that this
was enticing to "shrewd politicians." What simple political computation could add the number of potential
Negro voters to be derived from a minority population
that reached a high of 3.4 per cent in New Jersey and
2.4 per cent in Ohio . . . and predict a balance that
would ensure Republican victory? [30]

These arguments and implications must be dealt with in
detail. We have already demonstrated that electoral victory or
defeat in a number of crucial Ohio counties and the composition of the state legislature could be made to turn upon a
handful of potential Negro voters, if ever they were given the
franchise. The Coxes are mistaken to suggest that the voting
potential of Negroes was negligible because they comprised
only 2.4 percent of the population. The Republican party managers on the spot were fully capable of the "simple political
computation" that would predict a Republican victory if the
Negroes were enfranchised. The forecasts of Republican
leaders in Ohio on this point were clear and forceful. The

Mahoning Courier, for example, on April 17, 1867, remarked: "The Democracy of the North well know the power of the negro vote, should the franchise be extended, and dread it as they would a pesthouse. Had the Republicans of Connecticut a year and a half ago . . . been fully alive to the interests at stake, they would not have been called upon to suffer the recent defeat experienced in that State. The colored vote would have secured a different result. Ohio to-day occupies an analagous position."

Furthermore, an article in the Portsmouth *Portage County Democrat,* an Ohio newspaper, for August 7, 1867, showed the tremendous effect that a mere 6000 votes might have on the political fortunes of either party in Ohio:

> In the election of members of the House at the next election, a change of 3,000 votes from the Union ticket, as the vote stood in 1865, will change the political complexion of the House, while in the Senate the same change will be effected by a change of 3,622 votes. Deducting from the last number of the votes of those counties included in the House estimate, and it would require but 6,035 votes to change the political complexion of both branches of the Legislature, giving the Democrats control of both Houses, a majority on joint ballot and therefore a successor to Wade in the Senate.

VI

On January 15, 1867, a caucus of Republican legislators met in Columbus, Ohio, to discuss an amendment to the state constitution which would eliminate a proviso that only "white adult males" could vote in Ohio. Most of these legislators were in favor of submitting this amendment to a referendum of the people in the forthcoming autumn elections. However, they encountered strong opposition from representatives of the southern districts of the state, who felt the amendment was "premature" and "unwise." [31]

On March 1, 1867, the proposed amendment was introduced in the Ohio House of Representatives and defeated by a
vote of 50 to 38. It was clear that the House of Representatives
was not prepared to sanction any proposal that might lead to
the enfranchisement of Negroes in the state of Ohio. Moreover, all 23 of the Republicans who voted to reject the amendment represented southern districts of the state. As a result
of their action, these Republican legislators from southern
Ohio were attacked by their colleagues in the north in the most
severe terms. The *Portage County Democrat,* for example, on
March 6, 1867, commented: "It is mortifying to be obliged to
put on record such action. . . . Men representing negro hating
counties voted against the amendment to retain political considerations at home. . . . These political tricksters and dodgers
will be hoist by their own petard. It is but a question of time."

Meanwhile, however, a similar amendment had been introduced into the Ohio State Senate. It was adopted by a vote
of 23 to 11 on March 27. In this case the amendment was approved by a strict party vote, for all the 23 votes in its favor
were cast by Republicans.[32] The amendment was then sent to
the House of Representatives.

The amendment was passed in the House on April 3 by a
strict party vote. It is of vital significance, for, among other
things, it indicated that Republicans had discovered a way out
of the impasse that had threatened to cripple their party for
years past. It was clear that definite and even brutal decisions
had been imposed upon Republicans in the House of Representatives for the sake of party unity. Many Republican
leaders in Ohio were overjoyed by the action of the House.
These Republicans were anxious to present the thorny subject
of Negro voting to the electorate for a final settlement.[33]

We must take notice of the fact that the House tacked a
second provision onto the Senate proposal. Those white voters
who had given aid to the Confederacy during the war or who
had deserted from the Union army were to be disfranchised.
This second provision eliminated the Republican opposition to
the original proposal, for Republican politicians had linked

two separate issues—the issue of Negro enfranchisement and the entirely different one of disfranchising those whites who might be expected to vote against their party.

By the terms of this second provision Republican election officials in the various counties would be empowered to declare certain whites ineligible to vote. These election officials could be relied upon to root out those white voters who might turn against the party because of the enfranchisement of Negroes.[34] These men were dedicated to their tasks not merely because of party loyalty, but also for more selfish reasons. They were well aware they would lose all the spoils and emoluments of office whenever the Democrats took over. They knew the electors in each of these counties almost to a man and could challenge those whose allegiance to the Republican party was suspect, and any Democrats as well.

The Democrats, for their part, spoke out against this feature of the amendment in angry tones. The *Portsmouth Times* on July 13, 1867, declared: "The Radical Negro suffragettes pretend to be in favor of a liberal franchize system, but we find they apply it only to the colored man, desiring rather to restrict than extend the rights of white men." The *Cleveland Plain Dealer* on April 8, 1867, commented: "This Radical party are looking to make the negroes the equals of white men, and through the machinery of their secret order and their party organization, to place the former above the white man, by giving the blacks unrestricted suffrage, and restricting it in the case of the whites, particularly those of foreign descent."

It thus seems clear that to divorce the question of Negro enfranchisement from that of white disfranchisement in Northern states like Ohio is perhaps to be guilty of a misreading of the political situation in that period of history. Those who write of American history in the late nineteenth century have told us a great deal about the disfranchisement of Negroes in the South as an instrument of political control. We should notice, however, that disfranchisement was confined neither to Negroes nor to the South.

The maneuver on April 3 in the Ohio House of Representatives was designed to accomplish two objects for the Republican party. In the first place, if the amendment were accepted by the people of their state, the party would be assured of the votes of those 10,000 Negro males who lived in Ohio. Furthermore, the second provision, designed to disfranchise those whites who might reasonably be expected to object to Negro suffrage, would protect the Republican party from any "white backlash." There may have been some "political risk" to be run in connection with the actions of the Republican party, but the second provision provided the Republicans with a means of limiting these risks by eliminating any white voters who might have tried to strike back at the party because of its Negro policy. The *Portsmouth Times* declared on April 13, 1867: "The Radicals have decided to bolster up the amendment . . . in the belief that this would induce some of the 'overly' loyal to vote for the amendment, who are opposed to the negro suffrage part of it." On April 4, 1867, the *Cincinnati Daily Enquirer* commented: "To suppose that these politicians [Republican] by trade were influenced, in this enterprise, by any other motives than those of a purely party character, is to give them a credit to which nothing that they have said or done shows them to be entitled." In the same way John Bloan, a Democratic member of the House, argued: "This amendment . . . limits the privilege [of voting] as regards white men, and extends it as to colored men."

Thus Negro suffrage, despite the Coxes, did not involve any "flirtation with political disaster." The two parts of the amendment, taken together, certainly provided the "shrewd politicians" in Ohio with a most "enticing prospect."

The disfranchising provision of the amendment was potentially a weapon of tremendous political consequence, for no less than 27,000 white men had already been classified as "deserters" by the United States Army in the state of Ohio.[35]

In fact, the number of "deserters" in the state proved to be something of an embarrassment to the Republicans. For one thing, the electoral situation in the state was so delicately balanced that the Republicans had no need to disqualify so many voters. More important, perhaps, some Republicans felt that they should resort to some other method to assure their majority that would be less severe than their "disfranchising" amendment, and thus win for themselves a measure of popularity even among those whom they were attacking. Republican leaders in Ohio urged this course upon their various congressmen. William West, the Attorney-General of Ohio, wrote to Senator Wade: "It will be a severe blow if some action is not taken with regard to deserters as suggested. . . . Very many of our best soldiers stood marked on the rolls as deserters." [36]

The technical status and condition of some of the "deserters" provided a solution to the problem. Many of these men were deserters only in a technical sense. They had fought for the Union cause but had left the army on their own initiative after Appomatox, believing that with the end of the war their military obligations to the country had ended as well.[37] They did not possess official discharge papers and could be disfranchised by the Republican election officials in Ohio whenever they deemed it expedient to do so.

Ohio's Republican congressmen secured the passage of legislation in July, 1867, that removed these "technical deserters" from that odious classification: "Be it enacted, That no soldier or sailor shall be taken or held to be a deserter . . . who faithfully served according to his enlistment, until the 19th day of April, 1865, and who, without proper authority or leave first obtained, did quit his command, or refuse to serve after said date. . . ." As a result some 7000 men in Ohio had this stigma taken from their records. The legislation had no effect whatsoever upon the remaining 20,000 men in the state who were still classified as deserters.

VIII

The plan seemed perfect, and the argument in its favor conclusive. It turned, however, on one point: Would Republicans stand as a unit in their support of the amendment? The answer was provided even before the campaign of 1867 began. Apparently, the results of the municipal elections on April 1, 1867, had a dramatic effect upon the loyalty of many Republicans to the amendment, for in these elections the Democrats won victories in three of the four largest cities in the state and in many other towns as well.[38]

The Republicans won the city elections in Dayton, but only by slim majorities in the various wards, ranging from only 150 to 690 votes. "A vast deal of scratching was done in all the wards," wrote the *Dayton Journal,* explaining the upsurge in the popularity of the Democrats. The Republicans carried Toledo by a mere forty votes. The Democrats captured control of Columbus, winning the office of mayor and many lesser posts. A Democrat was elected mayor of Cleveland for the first time in over a decade. At the same time in a number of small towns—Portsmouth, Fremont, Newark, Bucyrus, Tiffin, Circleville, Zanesville—the Democrats were elected to the most important municipal offices, offices which had been held by Republicans for years past.[39]

Many Republicans believed that their party had suffered this loss because it was too closely identified in the public's mind with the proposed constitutional amendment removing the word "white" from the state constitution. This feeling was expressed in the reports from townships that had been carried by the Democrats in the spring elections. The correspondent of the *Cleveland Plain Dealer* wrote about the elections in Columbus, on April 3, 1867: "Negro voting . . . entered largely in the contest" and, by the defeat of the Republicans, "was emphatically condemned."

As a result, significant numbers of Republicans now abandoned the very amendment that had been proposed and passed by their party in the state legislature and sanctioned at their state convention. It seemed to them that, unless they cut themselves adrift from the proposal, they could not hope to gain enough votes to win their own bids for political office. On April 22, 1867, three weeks after the spring elections, a leading article appeared in the *Cleveland Herald* on the subject of Negro suffrage and the Republican State Convention, which was scheduled to meet in June. The *Herald* advised: "There is no reason why the Convention should pass resolutions endorsing all the acts of the Legislature. There is no reason why the

Convention should notice the Legislature. One of these [acts] is the enfranchisement of the blacks. Lay that down, without regard to what the Legislature has done, or has not done."

In some cases, Republican candidates for office simply refused to discuss the amendment or even to refer to it in their political speeches. In other cases, the local campaign committees issued circulars which made it plain that neither Republican candidates nor those who had voted for the party in the past were obliged to support the constitutional amendment in the October elections. In a resolution adopted at their county convention in July, for example, the Republicans of Brown County declared: "We do not believe the Constitutional Amendment proposed by OUR last Legislature should be made a party question, but left for Union men to vote upon as they may choose without PREJUDICING THEIR STANDING IN THE PARTY." The Republican press also turned away. The *Cleveland Leader,* which had initiated the campaign for Negro voting in Ohio in 1865, now abandoned the issue in order to concentrate upon the Republican control of the state legislature. On July 13, 1867, the *Leader* declared: "The real contest at the coming State election will be for the control of the Legislature."

Thus, a crack appeared once again in the solid Republican front—almost at the very moment that front had been formed.

IX

Because of the new rift, the various factions of the party became more and more active, as early as April of 1867.[40] And again, these partisans were so jealous of each other that they were willing to sacrifice the entire party if they thought they could thwart a rival Republican faction.

One of the factions was composed of ex-Democrats led by Edwin Cowles, the Cleveland newspaper editor. (This group, you may recall, first proposed the program for Negro suffrage in Ohio.) He and his friends now had several goals in mind. They desired to win the Republican nomination for governor of Ohio for Benjamin Cowen, a former adjutant general of the state. They hoped to control and influence the election of Ohio's next United States senator. Finally, they planned to throw the support of the Ohio delegation at the next Republican National Convention behind Salmon P. Chase, who was their candidate for the party's nominee for the presidency. Salmon Chase, for his part, was prepared to join with the Cowles faction in this scheme. On March 28, 1867, Chase wrote to Cowen: "Nothing would give me more satisfaction than to see your name listed among the number of my supporters. Would you accept the nomination? It is I presume too early to do more than talk about the representation of Ohio in the next national convention." [41]

These ex-Democrats were bitterly opposed by the Republican party regulars, who were mostly ex-Whigs. They preferred to see the party select Benjamin F. Wade, the senior senator from Ohio, as its nominee for the presidency. They backed Rutherford B. Hayes as their candidate for the governor of the state. Above all else they were determined to thwart Chase's ambitions, because he was still suspect in their minds for a variety of strongly held reasons we have already touched upon in the first chapter.[42]

The Coalitionists were led by Senator John Sherman and by William Dennison, a former postmaster general of the United States. They hoped to build an organization in Ohio that could win the support of Republicans, dissident Democrats, and any other local factions that might be induced to join them. They already enjoyed powerful support in the press of Ohio. The *Cincinnati Commercial,* the *Ohio State Journal,* and the *Cleveland Herald* all endorsed the Sherman-Dennison combination.[43] Their chief object was to support Salmon P. Chase and to hamper Benjamin F. Wade in his designs upon the nomination for the presidency.

The political maneuvering was begun by the ex-Democrats and their leader, Edwin Cowles. Cowles brought up the issue of Negro suffrage to rally men to Chase's support and to organize them into a cohesive group. The regulars countered by persuading Rutherford B. Hayes, congressman from the second congressional district, to come forward as a candidate for the nomination for governor. In July, 1867, William Smith wrote to a Chase opponent: "The situation for Hayes is admirable. . . . Some foolish men in the interest of Gov. Chase and others are endeavoring to complicate the matter with presidential politics, but I have answered this effectively. Cowen is as bitter as death against Gen. Hayes and me, and threatens everlasting vengeance. His friends will seek to effect a combination against Gen. Hayes, but that will fail. . . . This letter is confidential." There could be no doubt that he would easily beat Benjamin Cowen, the ex-Democrats' candidate for the post, and thus inflict a severe defeat upon the entire company of Chase supporters in Ohio. (See Chapter Five.)

Much turned upon the outcome of the rivalry between Hayes and Cowen. The man who won the nomination for the governorship would determine, in many cases, the kind of Republicans who would be nominated for the state legislature, which in its turn would select the United States senator for Ohio. If Hayes won the nomination for governor, it would thus ensure the success of Benjamin Wade, the choice of the party regulars. If Cowen won, the Chase faction would be in a position to overthrow Wade and put forward one of their own number for Wade's place in the Senate.

Wade was informed by A. E. Candle on June 14, 1867, of the importance of the state elections in the fall. As one political friend told him: "This [the governorship] may be regarded as only a question of Ohio politics but in reality, it has a much wider significance. No less than a struggle for the Presidency on the part of Gov. Chase and his friends to carry the state of Ohio over yourself. . . . The Chief Justice seems more determined than he did in 1864."

If Wade were beaten, one of Salmon P. Chase's bitterest foes would be removed from active politics and Chase's chances at the Republican National Convention of 1868 correspondingly improved. On June 6, 1867, William Smith wrote his closest political advisor, Joseph Barrett, concerning this: "In conclusion, let me assure you that this is the beginning of the Presidential battle for 1868, and if the opposition are victorious, the state will support Mr. Chase in the next National Convention."

At the Republican State Convention during June, 1867, the issue of Negro suffrage suffered yet another defeat. The Republican factions at the convention were able to agree neither upon measures nor upon men. Also, Hayes won the nomination for governor because the ex-Democrats split into several factions and were unable to gather enough support for any of their candidates, including Cowen. Some of Cowen's supporters remained with him through the final ballot; others, however, switched to Samuel Galloway and a few to Hayes.[44]

Hayes suddenly found himself the target of a savage attack by the Cowles-Cowen faction of the Republican party after he had won the nomination. This is borne out by a letter William Smith wrote to Joseph Barrett in November, 1867. "He [Cowen] took the extraordinary course, when he found Gen. Hayes was a candidate for the nomination before our convention, of avowing himself his implacable enemy and the enemy of all who chose to support him. He circulated lies about Gen. Hayes and resorted to every trick and mean act at the time of the convention to effect his defeat; when disappointed there, he proclaimed through his nearest friend that now he 'should lay back and go to cutting throats.' " [45] Cowen's attack was particularly effective because he was chairman of the Republican Executive Committee in the state. He thus was responsible for the organization of the 1867 Republican campaign, and he did not hesitate, in his anger and resentment, to use his position to defeat the electoral chances of his own party. (See Chapter One.) He saw to it that none of the many Republican speakers upon the issue of Negro suffrage were assigned in key areas.[46] As a result of Cowen's tactics, some contests were lost by default, and the Republicans lost their control of the state legislature. Hayes was only elected governor by a majority of 2848 votes. In addition, the amendment was defeated by a majority of over 50,000 votes.

It is a singular comment upon the politics of the time that the very men who had brought the issue of Negro suffrage to the front in 1865 were responsible for its decisive defeat only two years later. Many Republican newspapers described the politics of the time clearly. The *Summit County Beacon,* for example, on November 14, 1867, declared: "The people are tired of this continual chaffing, bickering, scheming, and trickery, of partisan interference for purely selfish ends. . . ."

X

The Democrats had gained control of the state legislature, and they proceeded to disfranchise certain segments of the public that might be expected to vote Republican. Like the Republicans before them, they sought to exploit the franchise issue for the sake of their own partisan objects.

A series of measures labeled "the purity of elections" was passed in April, 1868, by a strict party vote in the Ohio legislature. There were three of these bills: the Student Voting Bill; the Soldier Voting Bill; and the so-called Visible Admixture Bill.

The Democrats passed the Student Voting Bill because they assumed that most college students in Ohio voted Republican. Perhaps this was the case, for the *Columbus State Journal* for May 4, 1868, reported that there were about 400 students attending the local college in the town of Highland, but that "no more than 20 of all are Democrats." The bill was meant to prevent students from deciding the outcome of elections where the vote was so evenly balanced that a few votes could make the difference between victory and defeat. According to its terms, college students who were not residents of the area in which their college was located were not permitted to vote in local or state elections.

The Democrats expected that war veterans would also vote for the Republican party, the party of war and victory. Therefore the Democratic legislature passed the Soldier Voting Bill to deprive of the vote soldiers recuperating from wounds in hospitals who were not residents of the area.[47]

The Visible Admixture Bill was aimed at those electors who could not be classified as "pure white." [48] The bill permitted Democratic election officials to challenge anyone with a dark complexion or with "African blood." Anyone who was challenged was required to bring forward two witnesses to testify that he, his parents, and his grandparents were all "pure white." Those who were challenged also had to fill out a questionnaire that was so intricate and complex that many could not furnish adequate replies. (The Ohio Supreme Court declared the bill unconstitutional on June 3, 1868.)

Meanwhile, the Republicans turned to the Federal Congress for a measure of some kind that could finally remove the issue of Negro suffrage from the local and national political scene.[49] The Fifteenth Amendment was passed by the Congress of the United States in February, 1869, as a result of Republican pressure. According to the terms of the Fifteenth Amendment no citizen of the United States could be denied the franchise on account of race, creed, or color.

The Republicans realized at once that the Fifteenth Amendment did not guarantee the suffrage to the Negro.[50] A leading article in the *Cincinnati Daily Gazette* for January 29, 1869, declared: "The action is a decided rejection of the principle of establishing equal male suffrage by the Constitution. . . . This [Fifteenth Amendment] still recognized the power of each State to disfranchise citizens by any rule of disqualifications which did not make either race or color or want of property or of education a cause." State governments could still disfranchise Negroes by poll taxes, literacy tests, or property taxes. Nevertheless the Republicans felt that even if Negroes were disfranchised in the Southern states, their votes might serve as the decisive factor in many Northern states. The Republicans welcomed the Amendment, for, as a decision of the federal legislature, it would relieve them of the grievous burden of the issue of Negro suffrage.[51]

The state legislature in Ohio had to decide on the ratification of the amendment. The bill was first submitted at the same time the state elections of 1868 had taken place, one result of which had been the election of seven legislators from the Reform party who upset the balance between Democrats and Republicans. (The Reform party was composed of Republicans who could not countenance the graft and corruption which dominated their party's politics and Democrats who objected to the principal policies of their party.) These new legislators voted for ratification, and their votes were enough to turn the balance in favor of the amendment.

In summary, Negroes in Ohio were permitted to vote, but many of the politicians actually were little concerned with the fate and future of the Negro people in the life of their state and the country. The Republicans were mainly interested, as they had been for years past, in advancing the cause of one Republican faction or another. The issue of Negro suffrage was merely another question that might be exploited to further the fortunes of one group within the party or to plague and hamper the activities of another. A high point in these developments was reached, as we saw, in 1867, when the very men who had been responsible for bringing the Negro question to the front in Ohio politics abandoned the Negro cause for no other reason save that of factional tactics and advantages.

Republicans and Democrats were really interested in disfranchising any elements, Negro or white, that might vote for the other side. The Republicans tried to take the vote away from voters in Democratic strongholds in 1867, and the Democrats sought to take the vote away from those groups or classes of voters who might be presumed to vote Republican in 1868 and 1869. The factional battles which had distinguished the parties for years past did not dissolve in the face of the tremendous question of whether or not Negroes should be allowed to vote after the Civil War. Rather, the factions used the issue as they had used so many others for years past, and the pattern of Ohio politics remained as it had been since the very founding of the Republican party in 1854.

These conclusions suggest that much of the so-called debate upon the issues of reconstruction in Ohio was, in fact, a pseudo-debate, engaged in by men who were concerned less with great questions than with narrow tactics and squabbling, typical of political life throughout this entire period.

NOTES

1. Flamen Ball to Chase, April 16, 1865, *Chase mss.;* Earl Barrett to Smith, June 26, 1865, *Smith mss.;* Aaron Perry to Cox, June 4, 1865, *Cox mss.;* David Lowe to Bateman, November 24, 1865, *Bateman mss.;* See also *Portage County Democrat,* June 21, 1865.

2. William Coggeshall Diary, entry dated June 20, 1865, *William Coggeshall mss.,* Ohio Historical Society.

3. Cox to Aaron Perry, June 4, 1865, *Cox mss.*

4. See Ninth Census of the United States, 1870: *Statistics of the Population* (Washington, 1872), pp. 55–56. For a discussion of the growth of the Negro population in Ohio see James Rodabaugh, "The Negro in Ohio," *The Journal of Negro History,* XXXI (1946), 9–29.

5. Ninth Census of the United States, *op. cit.,* p. 56.

6. For a discussion of these "Black Laws" and the Negro's unsuccessful attempt to abolish them, see J. Reuben Sheeler, "The Struggle of the Negro in Ohio for Freedom," *Journal of Negro History,* XXXI (1946), 208–26.

7. Williston Lofton, "Northern Labor and the Negro during the Civil War," *Journal of Negro History,* XXXIV (1949), 256–62.

8. See, for example, the *Cleveland Plain Dealer,* June 20, 1865; the *Cincinnati Daily Enquirer,* July 28, 1865; *The Marietta Times,* June 22, 1865. See also Joseph Geiger to John Sherman, October 19, 1865, *Sherman mss.;* Oran Follett to James Comly, November 15, 1865, *Comly mss.; Columbus State Journal,* June 23, 1865.

9. Cox to Garfield, July 30, 1865, *Cox mss.; Cincinnati Daily Commercial,* August 11, 1865; *Mahoning Register,* July 5, 1865.

10. See Oran Follett to Thomas Ewing, May 12, 1854, Thomas Ewing to Follett, May 17, 1854, Joseph Medill to Follett, May 24, 1854, in *Selections from the Follett Papers,* Historical and Philosophical Society of Ohio, Quarterly Publications, XIII, 72–73.

11. We should be clear, in this regard, that in the prewar period these men confined their concern for the Negro to the abolition of slavery. Upon the subject of political and social equality for the Negro, they were either hostile or indifferent.

12. Larz Anderson to Cox, June 22, 1865, *Cbx mss.;* R. P. L. Baber to Johnson, July 4, 1865, *Johnson mss.;* Edward Noyes to Smith, May 30, 1865, *Smith mss.; Cincinnati Daily Commercial,* June 22, 1865.

13. For a discussion of the effect of the military upon the course of Republican politics in Ohio in the postwar period see Edward Noyes, *The G.A.R. and Ohio Politics from 1866–1890* (Columbus, 1946), *passim.*

14. See speech by John Sherman at Circleville, June 10, 1865, in *Cincinnati Daily Gazette,* June 12, 1865.

15. For Cox's attitude toward the suffrage reformers see Cox to Garfield, June 1, 1865, Cox to William Dennison, July 9, 1865, *Cox mss.*

16. Cox to Garfield, July 30, 1865, *Garfield mss.*

17. Cox to William Dennison, July 9, 1865, Cox to Garfield, July 30, 1865, *Cox mss.*

18. For the publication of Cox's letter see *Coschocton Age,* August 11, 1865.

19. William Painter to Sherman, August 30, 1865, *Sherman mss.; Cincinnati Daily Commercial,* October 6, 1865.

20. C. S. Mattoon to Strohm, August 14, 1865, *Strohm mss.; Cincinnati Daily Gazette,* September 2, 1865.

21. Richard Smith to Garfield, January 14, 1866, *Garfield mss.;* Charles Mattoon to Strohm, August 6, 1865, *Strohm mss.; Portsmouth Times,* September 23, 1865.

22. See speech by John Hutchins at Ravenna, July 17, 1865, in *Cincinnati Daily Gazette,* July 25, 1865.

23. See, for example, *Columbus Crisis,* August 2, 1865.

24. *Cincinnati Daily Gazette,* September 18, 1866. Other Republican leaders in Ohio argued that the protection of the Negro in his civil rights would not only be an act of justice, but would drain the Negroes in the North back to the Southern states, where soil and climate were "best suited" for the black man. See, for example, the editorial in the *Cincinnati Daily Commercial,* August 18, 1865; see also, for an excellent discussion of the use of this argument by Republican leaders, C. Vann Woodward, "Seeds of Failure in Radical Race Policy," in Harold Hyman (ed.), *New Frontiers of the American Reconstruction* (Urbana, 1966), pp. 127–29.

25. *The Portsmouth Times,* June 2, 1866.

26. For a discussion of this aspect of Republican politics in the period following the Civil War, see C. Vann Woodward, "Seeds of Failure in Radical Race Policy," *op. cit., passim.*

27. See, in this connection, the editorial in *Cincinnati Daily Gazette,* April 2, 1867.

28. Halstead to Sherman, February 22, 1867.

29. See, for a breakdown of the Negro population of the United States for this period, John Cummings, *Negro Population in the United States, 1790–1915* (Washington, D.C., 1918).

30. La Wanda and John H. Cox, "Negro Suffrage and Republican Politics: The Problem of Motivation in Reconstruction Historiography," *Journal of Southern History,* XXXIII (1967), 315–30.

31. See *Columbus State Journal,* January 16, 1867. For the debate between Republicans at the caucus on the issue of Negro suffrage in Ohio see *Cleveland Plain Dealer,* January 17, 1867.

32. Richard Smith to William Smith, March 20, 1867, *Smith mss.;* Henry Martin to Sherman, March 29, 1867, *Sherman mss.; Portage County Democrat,* March 28, 1867.

33. See, in this connection, *Dayton Journal,* April 5, 1867.

34. *Portsmouth Times,* April 20, 1867; *Elyria Democrat,* June 19, 1867; *Miami Union,* April 20, 1867.

35. See *Elyria Democrat,* April 18, 1867.

36. William West to Wade, July 10, 1867, *Wade mss.*

37. *Portsmouth Times,* April 20, 1867.

38. The voting returns for the municipal elections of 1867 from the

four largest cities in the state may be found in the following newspapers:
Cincinnati Daily Gazette, April 4, 1867; *Dayton Journal*, April 6, 1867;
Toledo Blade, April 5, 1867; *Cleveland Plain Dealer*, April 5, 1867.

39. For the voting returns in the large cities, see the *Toledo Blade*,
April 5, 1867; *Columbus State Journal*, April 2, 1867; *Cleveland Plain
Dealer*, April 3, 1867.

40. Benjamin Potts to Cowen, March 26, 1867, *Cowen mss.;* Henry
Martin to Bateman, May 9, 1867, *Bateman mss.;* C. S. Hamilton to
Comly, May 11, 1867, *Comly mss.*

41. Chase to Cowen, March 28, 1867, *Cowen mss.*

42. Smith to Hayes, January 29, 1867, Hayes to Bateman, February 9, 1867, *Hayes mss.;* Bateman to Richard Smith, April 21, 1867,
Smith mss.; See also Chapter Five.

43. See *Cincinnati Daily Gazette*, June 20, 1867; *Columbus State
Journal*, May 23, 1867; *Dayton Journal*, June 8, 1867.

44. For comments on this battle at the convention see Smith to
Whitelaw Reid, June 22, 1867, Smith to Joseph Barrett, June 29, 1867,
Smith to Robert Mussey, June 29, 1867, *Smith mss.;* Samuel Wilkenson
to Bateman, June 26, 1867, *Bateman mss.; Columbus State Journal*,
June 24, 1867; *Portage County Democrat*, June 26, 1867; *Cincinnati
Daily Gazette*, June 20, 1867.

45. Smith to General Schneider, November 2, 1867, *Smith mss.*

46. For Republican criticism of Cowen's behavior during the 1867
campaign see *Cincinnati Daily Gazette*, October 10, 1867; *Toledo Blade*,
October 11, 1867; *Dayton Journal*, October 9, 1867.

47. See *The Ohio Repository*, May 6, 1868; *Miami Union*, April 25,
1868; *Steubenville Weekly Herald*, May 8, 1868; *The Coshocton Age*,
May 5, 1868.

48. See *Cincinnati Daily Gazette*, May 16, 1868; *Toledo Blade*, May
6, 1868; *Cleveland Plain Dealer*, April 28, 1868.

49. See, for example, *Cincinnati Daily Gazette*, December 3, 1867;
Portage County Democrat, March 25, 1868; *Miami Union*, January 18,
1868; *Mahoning Courier*, November 30, 1867; *Steubenville Weekly
Herald*, November 22, 1867.

50. For this and other aspects of the Fifteenth Amendment see
William Gillette, *The Right to Vote: Politics and the Passage of the
Fifteenth Amendment* (Baltimore, 1965), *passim.*

51. Cox to Garfield, July 26, 1869, *Garfield mss.;* Williard Warner
to Sherman, March 5, 1869, *Sherman mss.; Cincinnati Daily Gazette*,
March 2, 1869.

The Politics of Plunder

CHAPTER FOUR

I

In the North Republicans found themselves in a difficult
position during the years immediately following the Civil
War. They had to face and deal with the complicated task of
reconstructing the Union. At the same time they realized that
much of their success in meeting this responsibility turned
upon the unity of their party, of which there was little. For
one thing, the Republican leaders battled with their fellows
over the distribution of patronage and the other gifts of political power. In order to understand the nature of Ohio politics
more completely, we must now examine this matter of patronage and the various issues connected with it.

During the reconstruction period the Republican party
was not the monolith it became later on. It existed as an
amalgam of local parties, each with its own leaders and objects
in the political life of the state. In these circumstances it is

entirely incorrect to measure the Republican party by modern standards of organization, unity of purpose, and decisiveness of leadership. As one Republican leader, Senator John Sherman, said of his party in 1865, it was a "maelstrom" and he complained bitterly of the inability of Republicans to work together for any purpose.[1]

This maelstrom existed for several reasons. First, Republican leaders, such as Thomas Corwin, Thomas Ewing, Edwin Stanton, and Salmon P. Chase, among many others, had either died, retired, or been forced out of office.[2] These men had exercised great power and prestige over the affairs of the state since the birth of the Republican party in 1855. They were being replaced by such men as Rutherford B. Hayes, John Sherman, and Aaron F. Perry. They were young and eager, but they did not yet enjoy the unchallenged power and authority the older leaders had. (See Chapter One.)

Second, the Republican party in Ohio was plagued by protracted struggles between its "ex-party" members that had begun soon after the establishment of the party in 1855. The most serious and significant of these struggles lay between Republican ex-Whigs and ex-Democrats.[3] The war effort forced the various factions to act together, but this cooperation between Republican "ex-party" members barely survived the war. Their hatred for each other reasserted itself during the state and national elections of 1864.

Third, the Republican party in Ohio did not possess the machinery with which to ensure proper discipline and give coherence to its political actions. For example, there were few accepted procedures to regulate the nomination of political candidates to state and local offices. Rival party factions could set the time and place for nominations to office according to their own narrow desires. No fixed rules set the time and place for holding primaries, and no regulation provided the means to determine what persons were eligible to participate in them.[4] The party did possess some machinery to manage its affairs. In Ohio, this was the function of the State Central Executive Committee. The agency, however, did not enjoy enough authority to enforce its recommendations. As a result,

Republicans frequently defied their party without fear of that kind of punishment that might have been meted out to them in a later era. Thus, Cowen felt he could perform the way he did during the elections of 1867. (See Chapters One and Three.) These weaknesses in the organization gave an intensely competitive and unrestrained character to the conduct of party affairs in the reconstruction period.

II

When the prewar balance of power between the two major parties was beginning to reassert itself in the state, the subject of organization and efficient management could no longer be ignored.[5]

James A. Garfield was typical of the younger Republicans who undertook to reorganize the party along more efficient lines. He had gained a reputation in the army that had made him a popular figure in his district, the nineteenth, in northeastern Ohio. A group of Republicans persuaded Garfield to leave the service in 1864 to run for Congress against John Hutchins, the incumbent congressman, and a member of their own party. Garfield received the nomination from his party and was elected to Congress by a large majority.[6]

Garfield's problem in the nineteenth district was obvious. How could he maintain his position in the party during the reconstruction crisis in the face of the opposition of his bitter Republican rivals? Garfield decided to take no part in the controversy on a national level, on the advice of his close political friends. (See Chapter One.) He voted with his party on nearly every other issue concerning reconstruction policy, a policy designed throughout to oppose President Johnson.[7] He was more conciliatory, however, in his speeches. He supported Congress against the President even as he called for cooperation and understanding in their grim quarrel. He defended the policy of political freedom for all men even as he argued that Negroes were not prepared to be given the franchise, except for those few who could read and write. In this way, Garfield sought to avoid becoming too deeply involved with this or that partisan viewpoint. In fact, in 1867, during the heated debate over military reconstruction and the impeachment of President Johnson, Garfield was in Europe. This trip, he explained to his constituents, was taken for reasons of health.[8]

At the beginning of his career in Congress Garfield began to study the problems of business and finance,[9] for he realized that these problems would come to dominate the attention of the nation and its political leaders in the years following the war. Also, he and his followers were certain that his knowledge of financial matters would strengthen his hold on the party after the crisis of reconstruction was over.[10] "Have noticed that you have directed your time and labor to financial matters rather than to general politics, and this is good," wrote one of Garfield's friends.[11] By the late 1860s Garfield had acquired something of a national reputation upon such matters as banking, money, and the tariff.

Meanwhile, Garfield worked carefully to build his own political organization in his district, based on patronage. He sought first to gain the support of the most influential Republican newspapers in his district by making the editors of the *Canfield Herald* and the *Portsmouth Democrat* postmasters and making the editor of the *Mahoning Register* clerk in the House of Representatives. He then secured from friends a list of the most influential and energetic Republicans in his district. He gained their support by arranging for them appointments as postmasters and tax assessors. "Our offices are now judicially arranged," Garfield was informed by a group of these officeholders.[12]

By 1866 and 1867 he made the acquaintance of influential men in various localities in his district. He asked their advice on matters of patronage and saw to it that their recommendations were listened to. In a letter to one of his political friends in the district, for example, Garfield wrote: "Can you send me two recommendations for a change in the post office at Basinburg. Both Wilson and Strictland are unknown to me as well as the present incumbent of the office."[13] As a result, their influence was placed at his disposal.

In his use of congressional patronage, Garfield was forced

to deal with very strong opposition from members of his own party in the nineteenth district. These Republicans were either rivals for Garfield's seat in Congress or disappointed office-seekers. Many were jealous of Garfield's influence in the district, and wanted to deprive him of it. On one occasion they obtained the signatures of certain residents in the district and petitioned President Johnson and his various department heads to remove individual Republicans from office. Garfield's enemies obtained the assistance of the Democrats, who were happy to embarrass Garfield and his party in the district. Garfield's opponents also drew upon a so-called principle—that of "rotation of office"—to demand the removal of several office-holders whose loyalty to him had been extremely effective in his renomination to Congress in 1866.[14]

Garfield's enemies were largely unsuccessful in their attempts to snatch patronage away from him. There is no evidence in contemporary records to show that Garfield's recommendations were not accepted during President Johnson's administration. Nor is there evidence to suggest that large numbers of Republicans were removed from their offices in his district.[15] On the contrary, from 1865 until 1868 Garfield's power and authority over patronage was almost complete, in part because he had the cooperation of Alexander Randall and Hugh McCulloch, the Postmaster-General and the Secretary of the Treasury, respectively, in Johnson's cabinet. Secretary McCulloch, for example, was very reluctant to interfere with Garfield's wishes in the appointment of Treasury officials in his district. McCulloch, for his part, constantly deferred to Garfield's selections and saw to it that President Johnson submitted them to the Senate for approval.[16] Even on the two occasions that President Johnson did remove certain Republicans from office in the nineteenth district, Garfield was able to select their replacements. "Nobody," Garfield wrote to George Chaffee in March, 1867, "can name an appointment in the district without my consent." [17]

Senator John Sherman had been elected in 1856, after winning the nomination as a compromise candidate. He quickly established himself as the most important and influential Republican in Ohio, as well as a political leader of national reputation.[18] He achieved this success by creating a disciplined political organization out of the many quarrelling factions.[19] He also enjoyed the advantage of having taken no serious part in the politics of his day, although it was known that his sympathies had been with the Whig party in the 1850s. Unlike so many other founders of the Republican party in Ohio, Sherman brought with him no bitter political legacies from the past.[20] He was to become a long-term supporter of Salmon P. Chase. Chase became Secretary of the Treasury in 1861 and Sherman was elected to take his place. Sherman helped build a "Chase organization" in Ohio to advance the Secretary's presidential ambitions. He signed the famous "Pomeroy circular" early in 1864 which launched a movement within the party to replace Lincoln with Chase at the Republican National Convention in 1864,[21] and he continued to support Chase in 1868, even though most Republican leaders thought he had no chance to gain the presidential nomination.[22] (See Chapter One.)

Sherman did benefit from supporting Chase, for the Secretary was careful to parcel out the offices of his department, one of the largest dispensers of political patronage, to those Republicans who wanted him to be president.[23] Chase relied on Sherman, among others, for advice on patronage; Sherman supplied Chase with the names of his own adherents. Those Republicans who benefitted from the system, in turn, became devoted to Sherman.[24] Thus, Sherman created a network of officeholders in every part of the state loyal to him.

Sherman faced serious opposition from his Republican colleagues, led by Richard Smith, editor of the *Cincinnati Daily Gazette:* Smith was joined by Benjamin Eggleston, a Cincinnati congressman, and William D. Bickham, the editor of the *Dayton Commercial.* These men desired to replace Sherman in the Senate with Robert Schenck, congressman from Dayton and one of the most powerful Republicans in southern Ohio, when the state elections of 1865 were held. They knew that, with Schenck in the Senate, they would be able to exercise a firm control over the distribution of patronage in Ohio.[25]

There was no significant ideological ground for Schenck's opposition to Sherman. These two Republicans had virtually the same voting records in Congress on both economic and political matters. Neither of them supported reconstruction policies for the South with which the other disagreed. Schenck's object, as Sherman realized, was to replace him in the Senate in order to enjoy the power and the prestige which belonged to a United States senator.

The movement to defeat Sherman's bid for renomination to the Senate was not successful, although he was renominated to the Senate only after a third candidate, John Bingham, released his votes to him. Nevertheless, Schenck's followers were hard and dedicated men who were convinced that their own power in the party depended upon their ability to drive Sherman out of its ranks. These men therefore continued to organize their forces in preparation for the presidential campaign of 1868, when they understood that Chase would again try to capture the nomination of the party for the presidency. Their principle tactic, in this campaign, was the use of political patronage to create a strong coalition in the party that would eventually clear the way for their triumph over the Chase-Sherman forces in the state. One of Sherman's political friends in Cincinnati, for example, informed him: "The scheme here (Cincinnati) is to put in power the clique with which your friends had to contend in the last Senatorial election—by controlling the offices in the city and county. They intend to use these officials' positions to place in their hands Federal and county offices for use at the nomination for President in 1868. . . . Your friends know of the activities of this clique." [26] This was state, as distinct from federal, patronage. They hoped that, with the help of those Republicans who had political offices to dispense in the various localities of the state, they would be able to elect their candidates to the state legislature. And these men, in turn, would be able to deny Chase the endorsement of his home state at the Republican National Convention of 1868.

Sherman realized he must reinvigorate and revitalize his political machine or organization in Ohio at once. On January 31, 1866, he sent a circular letter to his political friends in the state asking them to furnish him with the names of those Republicans in their localities who were sympathetic to his cause. He announced his willingness to accept into his circle those Democrats in Ohio who were prepared to break with their own party, as had other Republicans in Ohio, in order to join a political combination of which he would be leader.[27] He also proposed to exploit the third party movements composed of dissident Republicans and Democrats, who called themselves "Independent" or "Workingmen's" parties. Republican leaders in Ohio liked to refer to these various third party organizations as "Johnson cliques." Sherman's political friends in the state agreed with his becoming allied with these dissidents, but warned him not to become identified too closely with them. One Cincinnati Republican told Sherman: "Do not commit yourself too fully into the hands of the Johnson club or clique of our city. Some of them are very worthy gentlemen, some of them your good friends, but as a body they are not very powerful." [28]

Sherman also decided to use political patronage to strengthen his political machine. He therefore appointed several prominent Independent politicians to various federal offices in the state, among them three of the most important Independents in Cincinnati: Samuel Cary, Lewis Harris, and Bassett Langdon. They were made Internal Revenue agents in that city.[29] He also gave offices to Charles Sherman, his brother, Rush Sloan, his brother-in-law, Earl Bill, his business associate, and several others who were friendly to him, who then became his active allies. These men proceeded to select men, including some prominent National Unionists, to fill minor offices in Ohio. For example, after Charles Sherman was made a judge in the northern district of Ohio, he appointed Earl Bill as a court clerk. On July 26 one of these Independents, James Connell, wrote the following letter to Sherman's father-in-law: "My assurances of gratitude and thanks to Sherman. I will endeavor to retain his confidence and redeem my obligations to him. He can be assured that I will not forget a friend and that politically, I can both control and use power." [30]

Thus, Sherman's friends in the state were overjoyed. "I am gratified," Henry Martin, a "Johnson Republican," wrote to Sherman. "Your appointments were sparkling." [31] In 1866 many Independents joined the National Union party, created, as we have seen, to support President Johnson in his fight with his party over the issue of a reconstruction policy for the South.[32] They were called "Johnson men" or "Bread and Butter" politicians, by the Republican newspapers in the state [33] to make it clear that they only supported the President so that they could receive political and financial rewards. Some of these men were Sherman's closest friends and political advisors—men like Earl Bill, Rush Sloan, and Charles Moulton. They liked to refer to themselves as members of Sherman's "circle," and they had decided, long before 1866, to help Sherman in his attempt to increase his political power in the state.[34] Although it is certain that Sherman himself did not participate in the National Union movement, it is equally certain that he was a valuable friend to those Republicans who did. It is clear that Sherman supported these appointments for one purpose, to bring into his organization those Republicans and Democrats who were willing to place themselves behind his leadership in return for political office. In 1867, for example, Bassett Langdon, one of Sherman's cohorts, was appointed assessor in the city of Cincinnati. Langdon began at once to appoint several Democrats to official positions in his office. For this reason, he was attacked by the *Cincinnati Gazette* as a traitor to his party.

The correspondence of William Henry Smith reveals the anger of Sherman's enemies in Cincinnati over the appointment of Republicans like Langdon to positions of patronage in their city. "The Senate seems to be acting strangely in regard to confirmations, and is creating a good deal of confusion in our ranks," Smith wrote to Samuel Shellabarger on February 5, 1867. "Do the Senators propose to confirm a 'favorite' here and there—one recommended by some recreant republican—because he is of the same treacherous nature?" [35]

Sherman's tactical maneuvers and his "sparkling appointments" turned his original "circle" of supporters into an organization of strength and influence in the state. Samuel Reed, a journalist for the *Cincinnati Gazette,* wrote: "A sensational article could be got up on a list of all the Sherman family relatives that have fed at the public cribs. . . . The number would astonish the public." Another of Sherman's critics in Ohio described the Senator's organization in 1867 as "very formidable." Yet another Republican called Sherman's supporters in the state "the most powerful political ring in state politics." [36]

The leadership of yet another faction in the Republican party in Ohio at this time was in the hands of Rutherford B. Hayes, congressman from Cincinnati's second congressional district. Until the outbreak of the war Hayes had been a successful lawyer in Cincinnati. He had become a Union officer during the Civil War and was still serving when he was elected to Congress in 1864. This was his first experience with political office, although he had supported the Whig party in the early 1850s and participated in the founding of the Republican party in 1854, which resulted in his being elected to the minor post of solicitor for Cincinnati in 1858.

Hayes was firm in his allegiance to the Republican party. He could be depended on, more than most, to vote with the majority of his party on issues concerning reconstruction. He also remained cautious and circumspect concerning these issues. As a result, Hayes seemed to be the ideal candidate for the nomination for governor in 1867. His policy also prompted one of his correspondents in Cincinnati to inform him that "next to U. S. Grant you keep your mouth shut better than any man in America. . . ." [37]

Hayes remained circumspect concerning the issues of reconstruction because his party could give him little support when he was first elected. This was due to the fact that the party was divided into two hostile factions led by Murat Halstead and Richard Smith. The struggle between these two men was complicated by the emergence of the "Independent" Republicans, who had managed to attract some Democrats to their ranks. Hayes determined to build an organization loyal to him through the use of political patronage.

Hayes acted with cool calculation. He deferred to Richard Smith on matters of patronage in the second district. In 1865, for example, Hayes secured the appointments of William Davis, a correspondent on Smith's newspaper, the *Gazette*, as pension agent in Cincinnati. Hayes was accused in the *Cincinnati Daily Commercial* on July 29, 1865, of "screwing into all the petty little offices—City, State and National" the friends of Richard Smith. Hayes, however, received strong journalistic support from Smith and his followers at this early stage of his career.

Hayes also tried to establish friendly relations with Murat Halstead, the leader of Smith's opponents in the district. He maintained a regular personal correspondence with him and asked his opinions upon the most vital political matters in the district. Hayes also won the support of Halstead by carefully avoiding to criticize him for flirting with the Independent Republicans. (Halstead knew and appreciated their power and influence and wished to have their support against Smith.) Hayes remained silent even though other Republicans denounced Halstead as a traitor.[38] For these reasons, Halstead supported Hayes in his reelection to Congress in 1866 and in his bid for the governor's office in 1867.

Another example of how Hayes gained the support of both Smith and Halstead by his use of patronage deserves our attention. Columbus Delano, the head of the Department of Internal Revenue, wrote Hayes to give him a free hand in the appointment of Republicans to political offices in Cincinnati.[39] Hayes's reaction was to ask both Halstead and Smith to select those to be rewarded, but to preserve a careful silence about the matter.

At the same time Hayes took good care to avoid committing himself publicly to either of the two factions in the second district.[40] More important, Hayes remained silent upon the subject of the Republican schism in the second district.

Hayes laid the foundations of a strong, personal following in the ranks of his party, especially in southern Ohio. He enjoyed more support from the Republicans in the south than any other member of his party received.[41] Also, Hayes realized

that in order to fortify his position during the uncertain political times he could not afford to attach himself too closely to
any single group of Republicans. The details and significance
of Hayes's maneuvers at this time have been obscured by his
biographers who have said that Hayes was a man "above
partisan battles." [42] In reality, Hayes was very much involved
in partisan matters.

In summary, we should understand several important
facts concerning the political activities of Garfield, Sherman,
and Hayes.

First, it seems clear that in 1865 when these men first
began their climb to positions of genuine importance in Republican counsels, their party was in a state of profound disintegration and inner turmoil. We saw, in the first chapter of
this study, that the Republican party in Ohio had been plagued
by factional struggles in the period before the war. It is also
clear that in the years following the war Republican factionalism increased and intensified. Garfield, Sherman, and Hayes
were therefore forced, for the sake of their own political
positions, to concentrate upon building up groups or organizations of Republicans loyal to themselves only. These included,
in addition to orthodox Republicans, the Independents who
had broken with their party to establish their own independent
factions or political groups. Nor did Garfield, Sherman, and
Hayes limit their recruitment of followers to Republicans only.
They obtained the names of Democrats who might be willing
to join with them from their political friends in the state. In
some cases these Democrats were supported for political offices
in the various localities by the Republican leaders. As an example, James Comly wrote to Sherman on February 15, 1867:
"If any other Republican names come in for the assessorship
for this district delay action. There are good reasons why our
party interest will be best served by the appointment of one
of the Democratic candidates as against the others of his
party. I will show you when I come to Washington."

III

Students of the reconstruction period have dealt with the issue of patronage almost exclusively in the context of the struggle between President Johnson and his party. As a result, they have come to look upon patronage as a *weapon* that Johnson wielded over his party and to see the appointment and the removal of Republicans from office in the light of Johnson's break with his party. Perhaps they have been misled, in part, because Republican newspapers usually explained nearly every instance of change in the various political offices in Ohio in light of the quarrel over reconstruction between President Johnson and their party. In consequence, historians have assumed that President Johnson had a far greater role in the removal and appointment of men to political offices than he actually played, either in 1866 or later. The evidence from the political situation in Ohio shows that these assumptions are not entirely valid.

Republican leaders in Ohio were deeply involved in the distribution of patronage, and for a variety of reasons. For example, the Republican party was divided between the ex-Whigs and the ex-Democrats in a struggle for control of the district that included Cleveland. At stake in this contest was the postmastership of the city. George Benedict, the leader of the ex-Whigs, replaced Edwin Cowles, the leader of the ex-Democrats, as the postmaster of Cleveland. Cowles was removed from this position by President Johnson on the advice of Rufus Spalding, Benedict's ally and a congressman from the Cleveland district. Benedict nevertheless supported the Republican Congress in the split that developed between it and the President, even though he owed his appointment to President Johnson.[43] The defeated Cowles, however, accused Benedict of being a "Johnson Republican." He argued that the President gave Benedict the postmaster's job in order to buy his loyalty and support.[44] Later historians have tended to accept this facile explanation even though it is perhaps not an accurate description of what really happened. We saw, in

Chapter One, that it was Rufus Spalding, not President Johnson, who initiated the removal of Cowles from office.

A similar situation occurred in Cincinnati. President Johnson removed Alexander Sands from his office as assessor of the first congressional district in 1866, even though Sands was one of the most powerful and respected Republicans in Cincinnati. He was a political cohort of Benjamin Eggleston, congressman from the first congressional district, and together they controlled one of the strongest Republican "cliques" in Ohio. His own reaction was to publish a public letter in which he traced his removal to his refusal to support President Johnson against Congress. Sands' letter was quoted in the *Dayton Journal* on July 26, 1866: "I helped organize the Union party; I have done a good deal of work for it; I will eat dirt for no man, and no office will make me do it; The president may remove me as he pleases."

President Johnson did not initiate the removal of Sands. Rather, Senator Sherman had, for Sands had thrown his influence behind the movement to replace Sherman in the Senate with Robert Schenck, congressman from the third district. R. P. L. Baber, one of Sherman's supporters, took particular care to advise him, after his reelection to the Senate: "The *Gazette* continues its attacks upon you and I hope you will make them feel that the patronage of the administration don't belong to grumblers."

Yet another example of how the control of patronage motivated political struggles among Republican factions deserves our attention. Two Republican officeholders and political allies of James Ashley, the congressman from Toledo, were replaced by A. G. Clark and Dennison Steel in the spring of 1866.[45] Ashley denounced them as "copperheads" and accused President Johnson of appointing his supporters to federal office. Actually, the two supported the congressional position on reconstruction and were Independent Republicans. They were supported by William Dennison, the Postmaster-General.[46]

As another example, Horace Beebe was an assessor in the nineteenth district, represented by James Garfield. He was a political friend of Garfield's and an opponent of Johnson's reconstruction policy. He was removed from office in September, 1866, and he blamed President Johnson, although Garfield's enemies actually had petitioned the Secretary of the Treasury to replace Garfield's friends in office. On May 17, 1866, the *Cincinnati Daily Commercial* explained the reasons it felt Garfield was encountering opposition:

> Last winter Garfield took an active part in the Senatorial contest, favoring the election of Schenck. That, of course, was not relished by Sherman's friends on the Reserve. Then it was understood that Garfield proposed to succeed Ben Wade, and that General Shenck would help to draw reinforcements from Southern Ohio in order to do so. That did not please Wade's friends. So Garfield now has to confront the combined forces of Sherman, Wade and Hutchins, and it is not improbable that he approaches the termination of his political career.

John Sherman initiated the removal of Alexander Sands, the United States Marshall in Cincinnati, and William Davis, the pension agent. Both had worked against Sherman, and for Robert Schenck, the previous year. Sherman also was responsible for the removal of George Pullen as assessor in Cincinnati. Although Pullen was supported by Murat Halstead, a close political friend of Sherman's, he also had made the mistake of supporting Schenck for the Senate.

Robert Schenck and his followers also relied on patronage to entrench their positions. Schenck used his close ties with Secretary of War Edwin Stanton and Senator Benjamin F. Wade to gain his friends political office. As one example, William Nash had been very active in securing Sherman's reelection to the Senate, and Sherman had promised Nash an appointment to an office in the War Department in New Orleans. Nash soon discovered, however, that the office had been given to someone else. "Schenck does this," he wrote to Sherman. As Secretary of War, Stanton had a large amount of patronage at his disposal. Also, the Secretary was a political friend of Schenck. Stanton thus followed Schenck's recommendations over those of Sherman.[47]

Schenck and his followers also had Richard Smith removed from his position as pension agent in Cincinnati in 1866. Later that year Henry Martin, yet another of Sherman's allies in the state, was removed from his office as assessor in Toledo. Martin attributed his removal to the work of "mere partisan politicians," who acted under the direction of Robert Schenck.[48]

Schenck's assaults were not always successful. In March, 1866, for example, James Rothchild heard rumors that he would soon be removed from his position as postmaster of Findley, Ohio. He wrote to Sherman expressing his concern: "I have been informed that the son of P. Carlin is in Columbus making some effort to have me removed from my position as P.M. Carlin's son was opposed to you in the last election and was for Schenck. I have no doubt that this whole thing was under the influence of Schenck." [49]

Fortunately Rothchild was German, and the town of Findley was populated by a large number of German immigrants. Sherman was able to prevent Rothchild's removal with the support of these people, for their backing impressed the Postmaster-General to heed Sherman's petitions in favor of his protege and ally.[50]

The case of Richard Parsons furnishes us with another example of the relationship between patronage and Republican factionalism. Parsons was the assistant postmaster in Cleveland, located in the eighteenth congressional district, and in the congressional elections of 1866 he tried to win the nomination of his party for Congress from Rufus Spalding, who was the incumbent Republican congressman. Parsons was unsuccessful.[51] Nevertheless, Spalding was determined to rid his district of Parsons' influence and to pay him back for his opposition. He had Parsons removed from his office as assistant postmaster in the fall of 1866. However, Parsons blamed President Johnson, and not Spalding, for this personal disaster. As Parsons explained it: "The President may remove me as he pleases. I will eat dirt for no man." [52]

Certain Republican congressmen in Ohio regularly sought to buy off their rivals by providing them with lucrative official positions or jobs—either for themselves or for their relatives and friends. For example, Ashley was opposed in the congressional elections of 1866 by Thomas Commanger, a member of his own party, who ran as an Independent Republican. Ashley was reelected to Congress, but by a slender margin, and he realized at once that he would have to satisfy Commanger's hunger for office in order to eliminate his opposition in the congressional elections of 1868. The opportunity to do so arose in the spring of 1867 when Commanger applied to President Johnson for a position in the federal service. Ashley agreed to support Commanger's request provided that he accepted a federal office outside of Ashley's congressional district. Commanger agreed to his proposal. As Ashley wrote to John Sherman: "He [Commanger] will apply outside my district for a position. If he does this I do not want him damaged by having him rejected, but if he does not do this . . . then I want him rejected." [53]

William Lawrence, the Republican congressman from the fourth district, also used patronage to eliminate a rival. He was threatened by an "independent" movement in 1866 led by Donald Fleming, the assessor in the district. President Johnson removed Fleming from office as a result of the efforts of other politicians (who told Johnson that the people wanted a change). However, Johnson eventually realized he had made a mistake and promised Fleming another job. Lawrence promptly supported Fleming, and he was given a job in the spring of 1868, gaining Fleming's allegiance as well.

Republicans were sometimes forced to use patronage to settle disputes of a strictly local nature—so-called family quarrels—which were of no great concern to them. The Republican leaders provided jobs for some Republicans whose claims to this or that federal office seemed more valid than did those of others. They were forced to request the President to remove Republicans who might otherwise have kept their offices for the sake of keeping peace within the party.[54]

Some Republican congressmen, like Hayes and Garfield,

were newcomers to their positions, and they therefore had to use congressional patronage in yet another way. That is, they realized that they had no familiarity with some Republican officeholders in their districts who had been appointed to office by their predecessors. Garfield was determined to correct this situation. On March 2, 1868, he wrote to Frederick Kinsman, a political cohort in his district: "Can you send me two recommendations for a change in the Post Office in Bersingburg. Both Wilson and Strickland are unknown to me as well as the present incumbent of that office." [55]

On several occasions Republican leaders in Ohio actually supported the appointment of Democrats to office. This was done particularly by those congressmen from closely divided districts, where a few votes could make all the difference between victory or defeat for Republican candidates.

A good example of this kind of appointment occurred in Ohio's seventh congressional district, which was represented in Congress by Samuel Shellabarger, one of the most prominent Republicans in the state. Shellabarger was faced with the threat of an Independent party in 1866 which was composed of Republicans and Democrats under the leadership of Thomas Miller, a War Democrat, who wanted to take Shellabarger's place in Congress.

Miller, in turn, was opposed by some members of his own party, known as "Vallandigham Democrats," who resented the fact that Miller had defied them by supporting the war, in the period from 1863 to 1865.[56] James Comly, editor of the *Columbus State Journal,* and an ally of Shellabarger, wanted to encourage these "Vallandigham Democrats" to work against Miller. He, accordingly, persuaded Senator Sherman to support the appointment of one of their number to a state office. Judge John Dewey, an independent Democrat, was thereby given the position of assessor in the seventh district.

When patronage was involved many Republican leaders in Ohio sought the assistance of either Senators Sherman or Wade or Congressmen Schenck or Hayes. These men, in turn, usually made their various recommendations known to the heads of the departments in President Johnson's administration. Hugh McCulloch, the Secretary of the Treasury, almost always followed the recommendations of Sherman and Wade. Secretary of War Stanton usually cooperated most closely with Schenck and Hayes (who represented the southern portion of the state).

At the same time we should notice that Republican leaders in Ohio did not spurn President Johnson's assistance in matters of patronage, even after it had become obvious that a bitter struggle had developed between Johnson and his party. On April 2, 1866, for example, Edward Parrott, Republican Speaker in the Ohio House of Representatives, wrote to the President recommending the appointment of Lewis Campbell to a place in the President's cabinet [57]—Johnson appointed Campbell Minister to Mexico. Samuel Galloway, a prominent Republican in the state, wrote to the President requesting that the President allow him to direct his patronage appointments in Ohio [58]—Johnson refused Galloway's request. Jacob Cox, governor of the state, wrote to President Johnson urging the appointment of several men to office—eventually Johnson nominated all of them for various positions in the federal service.[59] The President approved the appointments of a number of men whom Sherman supported for federal offices. Furthermore, Rufus Spalding, congressman from the eighteenth congressional district, could write the President: "You did me a favor to direct the appointments of my friend Franklin J. Dickman, U.S. District Attorney, for the district of Northern Ohio." [60]

These requests to President Johnson were made with great delicacy and discretion, but news of their being made did get out and were condemned. Thus, the *Mahoning Courier*, on August 12, 1866, complained: "Garfield has succeeded in having the President's support in the appointment of his friends to political office in his district. He did this by making certain promises to the President on the adjournment of Congress at the last session. There has been much bargaining between Republicans and the President as well."

Also, the *Miami Union*, on November 3, 1866, attacked unnamed Republicans who had approached President Johnson "by side doors and back stairs" on matters of patronage.

What was the reaction of these Republicans to their removal from office? In their private correspondence these men were bitter and angry about the loss of their positions. They violently attacked those rival Republicans whose devious political maneuvers were responsible for their defeats. Almost all of these Republicans laid stress upon the intrigues and personal political ambitions that had resulted in their dismissal from office. Men like Alexander Sands, Horace Beebe, and Richard Parsons sometimes liked to pretend that they were thrown out of office because of their stout opposition to an ambitious President, and some historians have taken this facile view much too seriously. John and La Wanda Cox, for example, have argued that these statements represent the view of Republicans who "had taken a stand on principle rather than patronage. . . ." However, it was more often the case that battles over offices were begun by Republican factions in a power struggle with each other and that the President merely carried out their wishes.

Here again, it was not an overbearing President who exploited the patronage that was in his gift but rather it was the work of politicians at the local level who were defying their enemies and rewarding their friends by causing their removal or appointment to this office or that. In their public statements, however, these Republicans reacted in a different way. In public, they blamed the President for their misfortune. They argued that they had been removed from their offices because of their loyalty to the Republican party. They sought to make it clear that they preferred to sacrifice themselves upon the altar of principle rather than accept President Johnson's program of reconstruction. It was, we may be certain, a typical reaction of ambitious politicians. By these statements, these Republicans tried to put the best possible light upon their removal from office—one that might serve them well in the future. However, most Republican newspapers in Ohio preferred to place the blame for patronage changes squarely upon President Johnson's shoulders. They chose to embarrass the President rather than discuss the vicious political battles in the ranks of their party, battles which were more responsi-

ble for the removal of Republicans from office than they cared
to admit.

IV

The leaders of the Democratic party in Ohio realized at
once that the manner in which the Republicans were using
patronage could be exploited to divide their party. The Democrats claimed that the President intended to use his power over
patronage in order to force Republicans to support his policy
toward the South. They asserted that those Republican officeholders who refused to do this would be forced to "walk the
plank" by the President and be "swept" out of office [61] in
active opposition to his "radical" opponents in the ranks of
his party.

Although they supported him in his struggle with his own
party, the Democrats felt that President Johnson was first of
all a Republican (even though his general outlook upon the
subject of reconstruction was closer to their position than to
that of his own party). Accordingly, the Democrats empha-
sized that they were "spectators only" with respect to the
Republican schism, and that they had no interest either in
claiming the President as their own or in those federal offices
which were his to give by virtue of his position. The *Cleveland
Plain Dealer* published a statement typical of many on July 6,
1899, to the effect that: "The *Plain Dealer* is not the organ of
Johnson or 'any other man' except as he represents the principles of the Constitution and the Democratic party. The
Herald may keep the Post Office. . . ." Clement Vallandigham,
a prominent Ohio Democrat, said on June 22, 1866: "We
neither ask nor accept offices at his hand." [62]

Despite their remarks some Democrats wrote to President
Johnson to persuade him to appoint his own *"friends"* to
federal offices in the state.[63] Amos Lyman, a Columbus Democrat, was far more blunt: "The Democrats of Ohio want additional strength from you," he told the President on October
12, 1867, "for every Federal officeholder adheres to Radicalism.
They are thick here in Ohio and fought us everywhere. Remove

all the radicals and appoint your good friends. They ought to be made to give place to good Democrats. Great favor if I receive an appointment." [64]

On several occasions, sometimes in response to these requests and sometimes for the reason mentioned above, President Johnson did appoint a few Democrats to various federal offices in Ohio. He only appointed a few because he understood that the Constitution required that the President's political appointments had to be confirmed by the United States Senate, at least where positions of importance were concerned. The President realized that the Senate, controlled as it was by a Republican majority, would never vote for the confirmation of Democrats to offices in the federal service. Furthermore, most Democrats had every reason to avoid accepting offices from the President, even if they could have been assured of confirmation. They did not want to identify themselves in any way with an administration that had clearly lost the approval of the American public. (See Chapter One.)

V

What kind of men did President Johnson appoint to office in Ohio? For the most part, he appointed men who once had been members of the Democratic, Whig, or War Democrat parties and who had then joined the Republican party, as well as some Republicans, all of whom had then broken with the Republican party to establish third party movements. President Johnson took advantage of the fact that none of these men were any longer willing to support or cooperate with the leaders of the Republican party. The *Cincinnati Daily Gazette,* on August 17, 1867, described Johnson's tactics and motives: "The President does not appoint Democrats to office. He chooses, instead, the so-called conservative Republicans. He prefers men who have been Republicans and who, he fondly thinks, can do something to divide that party."

It must not be thought that President Johnson approved the patronage recommendations of Republican leaders simply because the wishes of the two coincided with respect to the appointment of "third party" men to office. On the contrary, certain of these Republican leaders received extremely favorable treatment from the President in the appointment of many "regular" members of their party as well.

This was the case, among others, with Rufus Spalding, congressman from the eighteenth district. As we have seen, in 1865 President Johnson responded to Spalding's desire in the appointment of George Benedict to the postmastership of Cleveland. From 1865 onward the President continued to favor Spalding by conferring political office upon several men who were allied to the congressman in his struggle against his Republican rivals in the district. Spalding's relatives, for example, occupied many splendid positions in the eighteenth district. In 1868 the President appointed A. W. McConnell, Spalding's brother-in-law, as chief revenue collector in the northern district of Ohio. On September 4, 1867, the *Cleveland Plain Dealer* summed up the patronage situation in the district by drawing attention to the number of offices held by the "fathers and sons, uncles and aunts, brothers, cousins and their descendants . . . of our beloved representative in Congress."

We must now consider to what extent the precedents and practices with respect to patronage in the postwar period differed from those of the war period. During the war Abraham Lincoln handled the patronage with great care and delicacy. As McKitrick has written:

> Important positions within a state were to be filled only after consultation with the Republican senator or senators from that state. Furthermore postmasterships were cleared through the congressmen representing the district in which the post offices were located. The dispensation and acceptance of patronage included intricate standards, a recognized punctilio, and a special morality of its own which was not lightly breached.[65]

That is, Lincoln dealt out patronage systematically and with method. Lincoln could do this, in part, because the Republican party won a sweeping national victory in 1860. As a result, Lincoln was given a completely fresh start at organizing the structure of the government, and he took full advantage of the opportunity. Of the 1520 positions the President had the power to fill, Lincoln appointed 1195 new people to fill them.[66]

Lincoln's appointments did cause some dissatisfaction. The beginning of the Civil War, however, imposed unity on the party and discouraged Republicans, who might otherwise have done so, from revolting.

Johnson used his power over patronage as carefully as Lincoln had, even when he removed those Republicans who opposed his policies in the South. That Johnson understood the limits of the power he held from patronage is indicated by a statement he made to Joseph Medill, editor of the *Chicago Tribune,* and quoted in the *Coshocton Age* on July 17, 1865: "If I turn these men out they would fight me like tigers; and those warm friends who pledge themselves to sustain my policy would cool down to few the moment I dispose of their offices." President Johnson faced a much different situation politically than did Lincoln. For one thing, Johnson could not completely revamp the government. Many people Lincoln had appointed were still in office and could not be removed, being Republicans, when Johnson became President in 1865. That is, Johnson could not make appointments as systematically as Lincoln could. The *Cleveland Plain Dealer* on February 7, 1867, announced that only one of every six Republican officeholders had been replaced. (During his tenure Johnson removed only 903 men of the total of 2934 employed under patronage.)[67]

Johnson's appointments also caused dissatisfaction partly because he had to replace Republicans with other Republicans, thus disappointing those in the party who were thrown out and also those aspirants who failed to secure office in the general reshuffling of places. Johnson, however, could not make appointments knowing his party was united behind him, for the war had ended and the party had promptly broken up into roughly the same old factions that had existed before the war. Johnson's use of patronage did make the factional quarrels more heated and bitter than they were or could be under the circumstances of Lincoln's administration.

Johnson also faced greater difficulties than Lincoln over the distribution of patronage because the number of jobs subject to Presidential appointment had grown so large that no single man could administer it, much less distinguish friend from foe.[68] In addition, Lincoln could safely rely on the advice of Republican congressmen concerning appointments. Johnson could not because the party had turned against him, and he therefore was forced to rely on the opinions of many men who held office on the local level.

VII

In summary, the "spoils of office" were for the most part controlled by the state leaders and they were primarily concerned with keeping control over the spoils. A leading article in the Democratic *Cincinnati Daily Enquirer* on March 13, 1867, explained the true state of affairs: "It is clique against clique—it is one set of party tricksters and managers against another—who only consult their individual interests." Warner Bateman, Republican leader in the Ohio House of Representatives, reaffirmed these beliefs. He stated that his party had paid less attention to the genuine problems of the party than to an undignified clutching after offices and places "to form the machinery of political and personal influence." [69] Henry Martin, a Republican of some prominence in Ohio, argued that the "highest aims" of his colleagues, so far as he could determine, were "self and self only" for which purpose the issues of the day were of little significance, compared to the distribution of patronage.[70]

There can be no doubt that "intrigue for personal ends" explains much of the bitterness that existed between Republicans, including President Johnson. We should not think that Republicans were angry because he used patronage against their party. What really angered them was the fact that they themselves had failed to benefit from the distribution of patronage while others had benefitted only too well.

In Ohio, John Sherman, Rufus Spalding, James Garfield, and John Bingham benefitted from patronage. They developed support for themselves by creating "auxiliary rings" and by giving patronage carefully in order to prevent their Republican enemies from destroying them. They drew men from all factions of the party—ex-Whig, ex-Democrat, and Independent. Ironically, to protect themselves, these men had to cooperate with the man who most hated their party—President Andrew Johnson.

NOTES

1. John Sherman to William Sherman, August 9, 1867, *William Sherman mss.*

2. For a discussion of this development see Evert B. Greene, *Some Aspects of Politics in the Middle West, 1860–1872* (Madison, 1912).

3. See, for example, the following letters to these Republicans on this point: A. Walker to Garfield, May 29, 1868, *Garfield mss.;* William Johnson to Hayes, March 17, 1868, *Hayes-Johnson mss.,* Ohio Historical Society.

4. For Republican complaints over these conditions see *Mahoning Courier,* October 23, 1865, May 29, 1867; *Cleveland Leader,* August 10, 1867; *Miami Union,* August 16, 1866; *Cincinnati Daily Gazette,* March 17, 1869.

5. See, for example, Samuel Shellabarger to Comly, July 25, 1866, *Comly mss.;* Chase to Cowen, March 28, 1867, *Cowen mss.*

6. For a discussion of Garfield's election to Congress in 1864, see Smith, *op. cit.,* pp. 276-78.

7. For Garfield's voting record in the House of Representatives see Glenn M. Linden, "Congressmen, 'Radicalism,' and Economic Issues" (unpublished Ph.D. dissertation, Department of History, University of Washington, 1963), pp. 102–104. See also Donald, *op. cit.,* pp. 86–94.

8. For Garfield's statement on these matters see speech by James Garfield at Ravenna, July 4, 1865, in *Portage County Democrat,* July 12, 1865; speech by James Garfield at Warren, August 22, 1865, in *Portage County Democrat,* August 23, 1865; speech by James Garfield at Toledo, August 26, 1866, in *Toledo Blade,* August 25, 1866.

9. Garfield to Burke Hinsdale, January 22, 1865, in Mary Hinsdale (ed.), *The Garfield-Hinsdale Letters. Correspondence between James Abram Garfield and Burke Aaron Hinsdale* (Ann Arbor, 1949), p. 73.

10. Harry Rhodes to Garfield, May 5, 1868, J. R. Swan to Garfield, May 22, 1868, *Garfield mss.*

11. Cox to Garfield, May 4, 1865, *Garfield mss.;* see also Benjamin Hoffman to Garfield, March 30, 1866, *Garfield mss.*

12. James Strickland, O. K. Walcott, Charles Lamberson, D. Dana, Andrew McCorkle, Robert Moore, E. P. Walcott, J. W. Lamberson, and others to Garfield, April 5, 1865, *Garfield mss.*

13. Garfield to George Kinsman, March 2, 1868, *George Kinsman mss.*

14. See Garfield to Nathaniel Chaffee, February 25, 1865, *Garfield-Chaffee Correspondence,* Western Reserve Historical Society.

15. This statement is based upon a close examination of Garfield's correspondence in 1866 and a careful review of the editorials of two of the most important Republican newspapers in his district, the *Portage County Democrat* and the *Mahoning Courier,* for that same year.

16. In this connection, see Garfield to Nathaniel Chaffee, January 17, 1867, January 31, 1867, December 16, 1868, *Garfield-Chaffee mss.;* see also William Outon to Garfield, October 11, 1865, *Garfield mss.*

17. Garfield to Chaffee, March 2, 1867, *Garfield-Chaffee mss.*

18. For a discussion of Sherman's election to the Senate, see Theodore Burton, *op. cit.,* pp. 57–59.

19. See John Sherman's comments on political organization in John Sherman to William Sherman, October 24, 1862, *William Sherman mss.;* see also John Sherman to William Sherman, March 23, 1863, in Thorndike, *op. cit.,* pp. 169, 214.

20. Burton, *op. cit.,* pp. 34–61; see also, in this connection, George W. Harn, "John Sherman," *Ohio State Archaelogical and Historical Quarterly,* XVIII (1928), 115–32.

21. Charles R. Wilson, "The Original Chase Organization Meeting and the Next Presidential Election," *The Mississippi Valley Historical Review,* XXIII (1936), 61–79.

22. John Sherman to William Sherman, August 9, 1867, *William Sherman mss.;* see also W. P. Denny to Sherman, October 24, 1867, *Sherman mss.;* Sherman to Warner Bateman, April 15, 1868, *Bateman mss.*

23. For a discussion of the Northern Civil Service and political patronage during the Civil War see Dorothy Fowler, *The Cabinet Politician* (New York, 1943), pp. 127–41; Harry J. Carmon and Reinhard H. Luthin, *Lincoln and the Patronage* (New York, 1943), *passim.* Philip P. Van Riper and Keith A. Sutherland, "The Northern Civil Service, 1861–1865," *Civil War History,* XI (1965), 351–69. For Chase's use of patronage as Secretary of the Treasury see J. G. Randall and Richard N. Current, *Lincoln the President: Last Full Measure* (New York, 1955), pp. 95–109.

24. For Sherman's close relationship to the "Treasury Officials" in Ohio see R. M. Stephensen to Smith, December 28, 1864, *Smith mss.;* Robert Smith to Bateman, February 23, 1865, *Bateman mss.; Cincinnati Daily Gazette,* January 18, 1866.

25. Rush Sloane to Sherman, July 22, 1865, *Sherman mss.; Cincinnati Daily Commercial,* October 6, 1865; *The Elyria Democrat,* January 17, 1866.

26. Allen Jones to Sherman, March 6, 1867, *Sherman mss.*

27. John Howard to Sherman, February 8, 1866, J. W. Keifer to Sherman, February 8, 1866, *Sherman mss.*

28. M. F. Force to Sherman, May 26, 1866, *Sherman mss.*

29. For Sherman's influence in these appointments see Samuel Cary to Sherman, April 27, 1866, Murat Halstead to Sherman, February 26, 1867, *Sherman mss.*, see also, for these appointments, *Cincinnati Daily Gazette*, July 14, 1866. For Sherman's part in the appointment of other third party Republicans to office see J. M. Connell to Thomas Ewing, Jr., March 27, 1866, *Ewing Family mss.*

30. J. M. Connell to Thomas Ewing, Jr., June 24, 1866, *Ewing Family mss.*

31. Henry Martin to Sherman, July 17, 1867, *Sherman mss.*

32. See, for example, the roster of the National Union party in Cincinnati, in *Cincinnati Daily Gazette*, July 20, 1866. For the roster of the National Union State Convention in Ohio, see *Portage County Democrat*, August 15, 1866.

33. *Cicinnati Daily Gazette*, August 7, 1866; *Toledo Blade*, August 23, 1866; *Dayton Journal*, September 23, 1866.

34. See, in this connection, T. E. Cunningham to Sherman, March 7, 1866, C. M. Moulton to Sherman, March 8, 1866, *Sherman mss.*

35. Smith to Samuel Shellabarger, February 5, 1867, *Smith mss.*

36. Samuel Reed to Smith, March 11, 1867, *Smith mss.*

37. William Johnson to Hayes, March 17, 1868, *Hayes-Johnson mss.*, Ohio Historical Society.

38. For the Republican attack against Halstead because of his support for certain independents see *Cincinnati Daily Gazette*, October 11, 1867.

39. Murat Halstead to Hayes, June 20, 1869, *Hayes mss.*

40. Hayes to Murat Halstead, February 2, 1866, Halstead to Hayes, July 6, 1866, June 20, 1869, Hayes to Halstead, July 18, 1869, *Hayes mss.*

41. In 1869, for example, Hayes wrote to Warner Bateman about the possibility of appointing an independent Republican to office: "I think it probable I can manage it, but at present can say nothing definitely. It is of small consequence in itself, and I like Col. T. but I must go in a straight path." Hayes to Bateman, April 19, 1869, *Bateman mss.* See also Barnard, *op. cit.*, p. 244.

42. Barnard, *op. cit.*, p. 245.

43. "I am pleased with your appointment here for Post-Master in the 18th district," Spalding wrote to Johnson. Rufus Spalding to Johnson, July 17, 1865, *Johnson mss.*

44. See, for example, the exchange between the *Herald* and the *Leader* in *Cleveland Plain Dealer*, June 27, 1866.

45. For the appointments of A. G. Clark and Dennison Steele to office in Toledo see *Toledo Blade*, August 23, 1866.

46. In support of Clark's confirmation, one Toledo Republican wrote to Sherman: "Clark has been faithful to the Union cause. . . . He has been . . . in the front ranks of the Union organization . . . in what may be called its radical element." John Osborn to Sherman, March 21, 1867, *Sherman mss.*

47. Simeon Nash to Sherman, March 25, 1866, *Sherman mss.*

48. Robert Smith to Sherman, January 20, 1866, *Sherman mss.*

49. James Rothchild to Sherman, March 20, 1866, *Sherman mss.*

50. David Locke to Sherman, April 12, 1865, *Sherman mss.*

51. See Robert Parsons to Sherman, March 8, 1866, *Sherman mss.* For Parson's attempt to capture the congressional nomination in 1866 see *Cleveland Plain Dealer*, June 27, 1866. For the charge by the *Cleveland Leader* that Spalding was responsible for the removal of Parsons from his office, see *Cleveland Plain Dealer*, August 23, 1866.

52. See Parson's explanation of his removal from office in *Cleveland Leader*, August 22, 1866.

53. James Ashley to Sherman, March 27, 1867, *Sherman mss.*

54. See, in this connection, Sherman to Bateman, January 19, 1866, Henry Martin to Bateman, May 9, 1867, *Bateman mss.;* Smith to Samuel Shellabarger, February 5, 1867, *Smith mss.;* A. E. Jones to Sherman, March 15, 1867, T. E. Cunningham to Sherman, April 4, 1867, Henry Martin to Sherman, July 17, 1867, Henry Kessler to Sherman, January 20, 1866, *Sherman mss.*

55. Garfield to Frederick Kinsman, March 2, 1868, *Kinsman mss.*

56. For the opposition of the "Vallandigham Democrats" to Miller, see Thomas Miller to Sherman, February 12, 1867, *Sherman mss.* See also James Comly to Sherman, February 15, 1867, *Sherman mss.*

57. Edward Parrott to Johnson, April 2, 1866, *Johnson mss.*

58. Samuel Galloway to Johnson, April 22, 1866, *Johnson mss.*

59. Cox to Johnson, March 23, 1866, *Johnson mss.* See also Cox to Johnson, March 12, 1866, R. P. L. Baber to Johnson, June 28, 1866, *Johnson mss.*

60. Rufus Spalding to Johnson, March 22, 1867, *Johnson mss.*

61. *Cleveland Plain Dealer*, June 27, 1866; *Cincinnati Daily Enquirer*, June 20, 1866.

62. *Cincinnati Daily Gazette*, June 23, 1866.

63. George Pendleton to Johnson, January 28, 1866, George Morgan to Johnson, March 20, 1867, *Johnson mss.*

64. Amos Layman to Johnson, October 12, 1867, *Johnson mss.*

65. McKitrick, *op. cit.*, p. 380.

66. See Carl Russell Fish, *The Civil Service and Patronage* (London, 1920), p. 189. See also, by the same author, "Removal of Officials by the Presidents of the United States," *American Historical Association Reports*, I (1899), 83–84.

67. Fish, *The Civil Service and Patronage*, p. 189.

68. For a discussion on this point see Frank J. Sorauf, "Patronage and Party," *Midwest Journal of Political Science*, III (1959), 117–19.

69. Bateman to John Sherman, December 7, 1866, *Sherman mss.*

70. Henry Martin to Sherman, April 11, 1866, *Sherman mss.*

The Presidential Question

CHAPTER FIVE

I

Two issues dominated politics in Ohio in the years after the Civil War, reconstruction and the question of Negro suffrage. Another matter, "the presidential question," also assumed particular importance in the political life of the state as early as 1865 when Republican politicians in Ohio began to press a number of presidential candidates upon their fellows. The result was party strife and bitterness which further complicated the conduct of public business in Ohio.

The names of several prominent Republicans were mentioned for the candidacy, but the most important among them was that of Salmon P. Chase, the Chief Justice of the United States and a former governor of Ohio.[1]

It must not be thought that in the fall of 1865 many Republicans had decided to oppose President Johnson in order to promote the presidential aspirations of Chase. On the contrary, many of them tried to work with President Johnson at this time and to put the best possible light on his policies concerning reconstruction.[2] It was only later, after the President broke with the party, that these men joined the ranks of those ardent Republicans who had turned against him in the early months of his administration. They chose to support Chase because they believed that his long career in politics, his service to the party, and his strong identity with the cause of Republicanism over the years were characteristics worthy of the honor.

For years past Chase and his supporters had tried, unsuccessfully, to capture the Republican nomination for the presidency. Such politicians as John Sherman, Robert Schenck, James Garfield, and Richard Parsons and prominent Republican newspaper editors such as Murat Halstead of the *Cincinnati Daily Commercial,* Richard Smith of the *Cincinnati Daily Gazette,* Lyman Hall of the *Portage County· Democrat,* and James Comly of the *Ohio State Journal,* made an attempt to get Chase nominated well before the convention of 1864.[3] (See Chapter One.) They helped distribute the "Pomeroy Circular," a document that sought to discredit President Lincoln in the eyes of Republicans in the North, among their other activities.

Men like Sherman and Schenck were convinced that Chase was in a better position to capture the presidential nomination in 1868 than he had been at any time in his political career. President Johnson was a Democrat. He had been nominated as Vice-President in 1864 to give the Republican ticket and the Northern war effort a bipartisan character that the Lincoln administration sought to promote. Only the action of a madman had suddenly thrust Johnson into the position of leader of the Republican party.[4]

Chase, in contrast, was a "regular" Republican. He had many powerful and influential friends in Republican ranks throughout the North. They felt strongly that Andrew Johnson was an "accidental President," who would serve out the years of an administration that belonged in reality to a "regular" member of the Republican party. After his first term ended they expected he would fade from the political scene. In the event the names of several Republicans were put in nomination in 1868, but that of Andrew Johnson was not.

Chase was delighted to learn that his political friends in Ohio continued to look upon him as the man who should be the next president of the United States. From May, 1865, to the end of the year, in fact, Chase encouraged their hope that he might be pressed successfully to accept the presidential nomination in 1868. In May, 1865, for example, Chase visited several states in the South with the announced intention of investigating the "social conditions" of the Negro freedmen. Within the month he was in Cincinnati, where he met and conversed with certain Republicans who had supported him for the presidency a few years earlier. Later, after his return to Washington, Chase took care to keep up a steady correspondence with influential Republicans in Ohio like Sherman, Halstead, and Garfield. To these men he expressed his loyalty, trust, and goodwill, and saw to it that even though he was Chief Justice of the United States his friends kept in mind the fact that he was also an ambitious politician.[5]

At first, Chase made no open declaration of his intentions nor did he permit his friends in Ohio to work toward a presidential nomination in 1868. By the spring of 1866, however, he became more outspoken with respect to his intentions. On March 16, 1866, Chase addressed a letter to Richard Parsons, a former postmaster of Cleveland who had managed his presidential campaign in Ohio in 1864. In it, Chase suggested to Parsons that the time was ripe for action. "Smith-Comly's father-in-law told me that you are too ardent, and manage too much. I mention this that you may be careful: but told him that friends who wait for something to turn up are the most valuable." [6] Chase grew even more willing to commit himself on the subject of the presidency; in October, 1866, he was told by Benjamin Cowen, the Adjutant-General of Ohio, that many Republicans in the state looked upon him as "our Moses" in 1868. Chase replied to Cowen: "I will not deny that I should be greatly gratified by such a proof of public esteem, and especially to the support of Ohio." [7]

Students of this period of American history have assumed that Chase wanted to be nominated by the Republican party. As his biographer tells us: "In the four years of his Chief-Justiceship, Chase had never lost sight of the Republican nomination of 1868." [8] Salmon P. Chase's presidential ambitions were not so confined, however. Indeed, the Chief Justice contemplated being nominated for the presidency not only by the Republican party but also by the Democrats and by a new third party as well.

It will be convenient to postpone a discussion of Chase's bid for the Democratic nomination and deal first with his third party activities. Certain friends and followers of Chase had approached a number of Democrats in Ohio in 1864 to suggest that they combine to form a third party in the state. For example, one of the Republicans, James Ashley, told Chase that he planned to establish a "permanent organization of War Democrats into a great National Party, which properly managed could take possession of the Great Government in 1868. . . ." Ashley believed that Chase could "easily organize a force in Congress" for this purpose.[9] If the new party should prosper in Ohio, it could then be extended to other states. Chase would become the leader of the new political movement that embraced both Democrats and Republicans, and it was proposed that he stand forward as the new party's presidential candidate in the 1868 election.

However, those Democrats who expressed interest in the scheme were not prepared, at this time, to leave their party in order to participate in the formation of a new political organization. They believed that they could exploit the disagreements that existed among Republicans on the vital issues of the day in order to weaken the party and allow their own party to return to influence and power in the politics of the state. Although these Democrats rejected the offer to form a third party, they took care to hold out some promise of participating in it, at some future time (see Chapter One), which explains in part why Chase continued to hold to the belief that a third party would eventually appear in American politics. Furthermore, he was convinced that when the war ended the various political elements that made up the Republican party would become disunited, encouraging the formation of third parties. His correspondence with his political allies in Ohio in 1865 served only to reinforce his opinion.[10] "Politics are wild in Ohio," Flamen Ball, a close political adviser wrote to Chase on April 12, 1865. Six months later, yet another correspondent informed the Chief Justice: "The politics of the State is getting daily more unsatisfactory. I do not see how it is possible for the present Union party to remain together much longer." [11]

The spread of such sentiments as that expressed by Flamen Ball did cause several Republican politicians to abandon their own party to run as Democrats in the belief that they had no chance to win with a seemingly disorganized party behind them. (See Chapter One.) Some observers were therefore encouraged to continue to think a third party could be formed in Ohio. Murat Halstead took a definite step to try to form a third party movement in December, 1865. He urged Republicans to form a "Conservative" party that would also include Democrats. He was quoted in the *Cincinnati Daily Commercial*'s December 26, 1865, issue as stating: "We have arrived at a new point of departure. The nation is saved. The war party as well as the Republican party has accomplished its mission. That new parties will arise who can question?" (See Chapter One.)

A number of strong third parties were formed in several of the congressional districts of the state. Some of these third parties, as we already know, called themselves "Independent" or "Workingmen's" parties. Still others adopted the title "People's" or "Popular" parties. All of them were made up of Democrats and Republicans who found it impossible to remain any longer as members of the two major parties (See Chapter Two.)

Chase seemed most likely to become the leader of a third party, as far as contemporaries could see, at the national level of politics. The Chief Justice "has great ambition and means to be President," Lewis Campbell wrote to President Johnson on August 21, 1865. He has "already made propositions to unite with the Copperhead Opposition." For his part, Campbell did not intend "to be thus transferred and kicked about in the market place. I protest that I am not mutton to be skinned and gutted and hung up on a hook over Justice Chase's meat block." [12] Other of Chase's followers in Ohio, however, were more enthusiastic. In October, 1865, Benjamin Cowen told Chase that both Republicans and Democrats would vote for him in 1868 because in "many counties" in Ohio there was "little difference between the two major parties." [13] Yet another correspondent wrote to Chase that the Chief Justice could become the great "popular" leader of the new party which would bring Republicans and Democrats together at both the state and national level. By July, 1868, Chase himself believed that he might be the "natural link" between the "great body of Republicans" and Democrats in the country.[14]

Edwin Cowles, editor of the *Cleveland Leader,* assumed the leadership of the "Chase movement." His real purpose in doing so was not out of admiration of Chase. It was to restore the authority of the ex-Democrats who had lost their domination of the Republican party to the ex-Whigs in the 1850s.

The ex-Democrats were very sensitive over their downfall, and the Democrats were quick to exploit the feeling: "Who at this moment occupies the most prominent position in the gift of the people," asked the *Cleveland Plain Dealer* on August 12, 1865: "Not sincere and honest abolitionists, we venture to say; but those renegade Whigs who have adroitly rendered the anti-slavery excitement subservient to their own selfish interests."

Other Republicans in Ohio understood Cowles' intentions as well. Lewis Campbell wrote to President Johnson in June, 1865, that Chase and his "earnest men" had embarked upon the "business of crushing." Jacob Cox, the Republican governor of Ohio, wrote to William Dennison, the Postmaster-General, that Cowles' object was to "break up our organization" in order to "ride" to the top of political influence in the state.[15]

Cowles began his campaign for Chase at the Republican State Convention of 1865. His first task there was to bring into prominence an issue that could attract a large following of Republicans who would also be loyal to Chase. He chose for his purpose the issue of Negro suffrage and made it the "test" of party loyalty in Ohio. On June 26, 1865, the *Cleveland Leader* declared that the Republican party should support two planks in its platform: 1, "The right of suffrage should be extended to the colored men of the South and 2, The State Constitution must be so amended as to give equal suffrage to white and black." (See also Chapter One.) Any Republican who would not accept Negro suffrage would be forced out of the party; only Chase's followers would thereby remain in it. Cowles was beaten in his design when the Resolutions Committee of the convention rejected his proposal about the Negroes. Defeated in 1865, however, Cowles continued to urge his plan in every part of the state as the one issue which all Republicans had to advocate if they hoped to enjoy the support of the party.

In his editorials Cowles argued that Republicans in their local conventions nominate for seats in the state legislature only those men who supported Negro suffrage. The *Cleveland Leader* declared on June 25, 1866: "Let us make our canvass on this issue. We assure our timid friends that this course will not weaken our ticket a particle. It will not defeat a single candidate—it will not drive away a single vote."

II

Senator Benjamin F. Wade was another aspirant for the presidency in 1868. Aside from the fact that he despised Salmon P. Chase and would do anything to thwart his ambition, Wade also realized that the nomination might represent his last hope for a genuine future in politics. That is, he was almost defeated in his contest to be reelected to the Senate in 1862 because a number of Republican leaders in the state had opposed him.[16] Although he won, the Republican leaders immediately began to discuss seriously the succession to Wade's place in the Senate. Those men most prominently mentioned to succeed Wade in 1868, when his term in the Senate expired, were William Dennison, Columbus Delano, and Robert Schenck. His enemies were so confident of preventing his return to the Senate that James Garfield, one of their number, could say on

July 12, 1866, that Wade would soon be "put on the shelf." [17]

Benjamin F. Eggleston was the leader of the Wade movement in Ohio and was a congressman from the first congressional district in Cincinnati. His friends included some of the most able politicians in the city and die-hard members of the "Eggleston machine," Alexander Sands, Henry Kessler, and William Davis. Wade also had the support and good wishes, early during the time he was trying for the nomination, of Richard Smith and William Dickson, the editors of the *Cincinnati Daily Gazette* and the *Cincinnati Chronicle*, respectively. Wade had few supporters, but they were active and outspoken, and their intervention in the matter of the presidential nomination caused genuine disorders within the Republican party.

Wade's supporters were primarily interested in securing for their group as much patronage as possible, which they could do if they could defeat Chase. Thus they tried to break up Chase's political organization in the state. Andrew Hickenlooper, an Independent Republican in Cincinnati, recorded in his diary on July 12, 1867, that if the Wade movement succeeded, the "Chase appointees" would have to "walk the plank." [18]

There can be no doubt that Wade was convinced, or allowed his friends in Ohio to convince him, that he could capture the Republican presidential nomination in 1868. This fact became clear to many Republican leaders in Ohio by two statements to which Wade gave his name in the summer of 1867. He delivered a speech in Lawrence, Kansas, quoted in the *Cincinnati Daily Gazette* for June 22, 1867. He called for the "redistribution of property" in the United States. He associated himself with the cause of the American worker, making a demand for an eight-hour day, for he was aware that the Workingman's movement had already appeared in Ohio. Wade, who had never shown much concern for the workingman in the past, now, of course, hoped to gain the support of labor. He therefore attacked capital harshly, as well: "There is an eternal struggle between labor and capital," he told his audience, "that will end only when the laboring men in this nation achieve that dignity which is due them." Wade concluded his speech with the statement that he had, during his years in the Senate, been a "friend" of the laborer.[19]

Wade had always been known as an advocate of Negro suffrage. However, on November 7, 1867, in a newspaper interview published in the *Columbus State Journal,* he took care to point out that while the right to vote was an indispensable part of the freedom of every citizen of the United States he, for his part, entertained distinct opinions upon the franchise question. He also told the correspondent of the *Cincinnati Daily Commercial,* in this same interview, that he was "a proper believer in State rights" and that universal suffrage was a "violation" of the "legitimate" functions of each state *in the North* to decide its own requirements on the matter of the franchise. Wade changed his attitude toward universal suffrage to win those white voters in the North who were opposed to enfranchisement of the Negro, and to further his presidential ambitions.[20]

Wade was forced to appeal to labor and to take a stand against Negro suffrage in order to gain the support of white voters because he was strongly opposed by Chase's friends in Ohio, so much so that they were prepared to see the Democrats defeat the party in the fall elections of 1867. The friends of Chase knew that state legislatures elected United States senators at the time, and they reasoned that if the Democrats won control, they would not vote for Wade, and his defeat on the eve of the presidential elections would adversely affect his prospects for nomination.[21]

Chase's supporters also launched a series of abusive attacks against Wade. Wade's followers, as a result, often ignored their Democratic rivals to counter the attacks of those who followed Chase. The struggle between Wade and Chase resulted in the Democrats' winning both houses of the legislature. Benjamin Wade's political future was terminated, and Negro suffrage in Ohio was dealt a smashing blow.

Wade was not the only major political figure in Ohio to have his career affected by the results of the fall elections of 1867. Some Republican leaders also believed that Chase's chance for the presidential nomination had been fatally injured.

These Republican leaders saw that Chase did not have a chance to win the presidential nomination, for he had continued to support the cause of Negro suffrage that his own followers had helped defeat.[22] More important, the Republican leaders also lost all faith in such leaders as Chase and Wade because of their campaign activities, while at the same time they deplored their "throat cutting" and "internal slaughter." [23] They suggested that a new leader be selected, one who had "fewer enemies" than any of the old leaders. They turned to Ulysses S. Grant.

III

Grant was not considered for the Republican presidential nomination in 1868 suddenly. As early as the spring of 1866 some Republican leaders in Ohio had urged that he receive the nomination.[24] The reasons for this early enthusiasm for Grant are not difficult to understand. The General was a national hero. He had never been identified with either of the two great parties in the state. He had never participated in politics. He had never taken a position upon any of the great issues of the day. "The feeling in favor of General Grant for the Presidential nomination in 1868," the *Portage County Democrat* declared on May 30, 1866, "grows daily in Ohio. If these feelings continue, Grant will be swept into the nomination on enthusiasm unknown in American political history."

Some Republican leaders in Ohio had serious doubts about Grant's politics, and felt his nomination would endanger their party. They knew that Grant had remained on friendly terms with President Johnson, even after the President had broken with the Republican party in June, 1866. Grant had also supported the abortive Philadelphia Convention, which the President had organized to oppose the Republican party in the congressional elections of that year. Moreover, if some Republicans believed that Grant's silence on the issue of reconstruction was a blessing, there were others who felt obliged to withhold their support from him because of it. These Republicans argued that the best hope for the safety of their party lay in a candidate whose political views, unlike those of President Johnson, were known and respected by them in advance of his nomination.[25] "Let us have a Presidential candidate nominated," the *Columbus State Journal* reported, "whom we know and can trust. . . . Better to be beaten with a representative man for a standard bearer, than elect another Democratic President. We hope the party will shun the nomination of non-committals— take nothing for *Grant*-ed, but know all about the principles of the man chosen." Despite this opposition, Grant developed strong support among Republicans in Ohio.

No one understood the fact that Grant was gaining popularity better than James Ashley, congressman from Toledo. Ashley had assumed the leadership in Ohio of a movement to promote Benjamin F. Butler, a congressman from Massachusetts, for the presidential nomination in 1868,[26] and Butler was eager to accept the nomination. Butler therefore had arranged to deliver a number of speeches in Ohio as early as the autumn of 1866, first to broaden the base of his support in that state and then, as a result of his appeal in Ohio, support in the other states of the North. On October 15, 1866, after Butler had campaigned in Ohio, Benjamin Cowen wrote to Salmon Chase: "Butler is in training for the Presidency. In the campaign in Ohio he was greeted in many places as the next President and loudly cheered as such." [27]

Ashley intended to help Butler in Ohio by introducing an impeachment resolution in the House attacking President Johnson, but actually to damage Grant's popularity as a Johnson adherent.[28] On December 17, 1866, Ashley proposed that the Judiciary Committee "inquire if any officer of the United States had been guilty of high crimes or misdemeanors under the meaning of the Constitution, or had conspired to subvert the Constitution of the United States." [29] Ashley had deliberately failed to mention President Johnson by name, and gave the congressional committee the broad power to investigate anyone. Ashley hoped to have himself named to a place on the investigating committee, and because anyone could be investigated, he would be able to "drag" Grant before the committee

in order to put the General's friendship with the President in
1866 in the worst possible light. If he were able to damage
Grant's reputation in this way, he would thereby boost Butler's chances of gaining the Republican presidential nomination in 1868.

John Bingham, a congressman from Ohio, saw through
Ashley's resolution at once. In the House, Bingham attacked
the Toledo congressman: "Specify . . . specify, name the thing,
Sir," Bingham demanded. The exchange between these two
Republican congressmen was recorded by the Washington correspondent of the *Cincinnati Daily Commercial* on January 28,
1867: " 'It's a stab at General Grant,' Bingham charged, 'and
no such malicious thing shall go through the House if I can
help it.' 'Suppose it does include Grant?' said Ashley. 'Can't we
investigate his conduct too?' Bingham looked at Ashley a moment and replied in a nervous wrath, 'Ashley, you're a fool.' "

The testimony quoted in the *Cincinnati Commercial* bears
witness to the reaction of some Republican leaders in Ohio to
the "intrigue" which resulted in Ashley's resolution. On December 21, 1866, the *Commercial* declared that the whole affair
constituted "the foulest, most malignant and most treacherous
assault that the ingenuity of devils could invent against the
man to whose valor and genius we owe the existence of the
nation to-day."

These remarks struck their target. Ashley was forced to
defend himself. Two weeks after he introduced his resolution
he rose from his place in the House. In an impassioned speech
he condemned the article in the *Cincinnati Commercial* as mis-
informed and inaccurate. He denied that he had desired to
harm Grant's reputation in any way. He insisted that he had
only "the highest regard" for the General and his achieve-
ments in bringing victory to the North. However, in response
to several questions from his colleagues upon the matter of his
exchange with Bingham, as reported in the *Commercial*, Ashley was evasive. Moreover, he refused to deny that such an
exchange had taken place, or that he had said: "Suppose it
does include Grant. Can't we investigate his conduct too?"

In spite of all his efforts, Ashley's motion was defeated

when the House refused to vote on it. Ashley brought forward a second impeachment resolution in the House on January 7, as if to clear himself of Bingham's charge. He impeached "Andrew Johnson, Vice-President and acting President of the United States of high crimes and misdemeanors." This resolution authorized the Judiciary Committee of the House "to inquire into the conduct of Andrew Johnson."[30] On this occasion, Ashley's resolution was adopted. Johnson was impeached by the Senate, but the impeachment movement failed, for in March, 1868, Johnson was acquitted.

IV

None of the various presidential aspirants—Benjamin Wade, Salmon Chase, Benjamin Butler—seemed to have much chance to win the support of the Republican party in Ohio for the nomination; the terrible defeat the Republican party suffered in the elections of 1867 made it clear to most political leaders in the state that Grant, instead, would capture the nomination in 1868. The *Dayton Journal* believed that the results of the October elections in Ohio were a warning for "all civilian candidates" to "stand aside" in the interests of Grant. (See Chapter Three for a discussion of the defeat of the party.) Such men as Robert Schenck, congressman from Dayton, therefore saw fit to begin to organize the first Grant "club" in the state, which he expected to become the principal force behind the Grant movement in Ohio. This movement did attract the support of several eminent men in the Republican party, including the editors of many party newspapers in the state. However, most of this early support for the General came from local politicians, especially in the doubtful counties, who argued with particular cause that safety for their party lay only in Grant's nomination, but who refused to believe Chase had even yet abandoned his hope of capturing the Republican presidential nomination.[31]

A growing demand for Grant's nomination soon developed among Republicans in Ohio. "What a rush for Grant," Donn Piatt, a Chase adherent, wrote to William Henry Smith on October 28, 1867, "and a very cowardly rush it is." [32] The *Cleveland Herald* argued that if Grant's nomination depended upon his support in Ohio, he would have "no serious opposition" at the Republican National Convention. The *Columbus State Journal* on January 31, 1868, declared that the General was "the most formidable candidate" the Republican party could nominate in 1868.

By the spring of 1868, it seemed to many of Chase's supporters in Ohio that the plan to nominate the Chief Justice was hopeless. James Garfield, one of their number, wrote to William Howells, the editor of the *Ashtabula Sentinel,* that the Grant movement in the state was "irresistible." Howells agreed. He told a correspondent: "The Republican party had put a padlock upon their mouths through the corners of which they squeal Great is Grant." [33] Nevertheless, neither Benjamin Wade nor Salmon Chase was willing to give up trying for a presidential nomination in 1868.

Wade calculated that he could win the Republican nomination if President Johnson could be impeached. (As we mentioned above, Ashley finally succeded in having a motion passed to start the impeachment of President Johnson.) Wade felt he could gain the presidency because he had been elected president pro tem of the Senate in March of 1867. This meant that if President Johnson were convicted and removed from office, Wade would succeed him, and achieve what he had little chance of gaining at the Republican National Convention in 1868.[34]

Wade's followers in Ohio realized this, and many accordingly supported the impeachment. The *Cincinnati Daily Gazette* reflected the enthusiasm felt over removing President Johnson from office. On February 24, 1868, the *Gazette* declared: "The inauguration of Wade will lift the country from the Slough of Despond to the summit of confidence, and will set all the wheels of national prosperity in motion. This is the prospect we have to make us hope for the success of impeachment."

Wade, for his part, was encouraged by these developments, and by November, 1867, there appeared definite signs that he therefore intended to challenge Grant for the Republican presidential nomination in 1868. As we have seen, Wade was prepared, at this time, to do anything in order to gain a substantial measure of popularity for himself. He now argued that Negro suffrage, at least in the North, was a matter of state rights. He called for the "redistribution of property," and became a champion of new policies to benefit the American worker. He deplored high taxes. He became an advocate of "reform and retrenchment" in the Federal government. Wade also began a campaign to undermine public confidence in General Grant. In several interviews with the Republican press in Ohio, Wade cast serious doubts upon the General's ability to preside over the affairs of the American people. On November 7, 1867, Wade told a correspondent from the *Cincinnati Daily Commercial* that he was "sorry" to see expressions of support for Grant. Wade professed to believe that the General "may be all wrong" both for the country and the party. In Wade's opinion, Grant could only be looked upon in the difficult political circumstances of the day as a candidate who might, if he became President, spend more time discussing horses than politics. "A man might be all right on horses," Wade declared, "and all wrong on politics." The trouble was, Wade added, the General had no party and no policies: he had only "shoulder straps," the Senator believed, and these were not enough to equip him to be President. If Grant wanted the presidency, Wade concluded in this interview, "he must not only be right, but must prove that he is. . . . If Grant wants the Presidency let him come out like a man and say which side he is on. The people want to fight political battles on principles."

Although many in Ohio supported the cause to impeach Johnson, as we mentioned above, some Republican leaders in the constituencies did not, and opposed Wade's candidacy. They were convinced that his nomination would result in a disastrous defeat for the Republican party in Ohio in the 1868 elections. They argued that Wade had already served twenty years in Congress. And they believed that he was too strongly identified in the public mind with the issues of the historic past. It followed, therefore, as one Republican correspondent wrote, that Wade's service to the party had now "come to an end." [35]

Furthermore, Chase's followers were opposed to Wade because they believed that his nomination would result in disgruntled Republicans' forming a third party, which was not idle speculation.[36] Actually, Chase's followers were primarily interested in seeing that Chase got the nomination, and they made it clear that they would prefer to see their party torn to pieces rather than cooperate with it in the election of Wade to the presidency. They denounced Wade without mercy: "Damn these abolitionists," one Chase supporter wrote in an effusion that was typical of the time. "I despise them." [37]

Out of fear that their party might be destroyed, and due to the opposition Chase's supporters generated against Wade, more and more Republicans began to support Grant. The Republicans, accordingly, chose Grant for the presidential nomination at the state convention held in Columbus in March, 1868.[38] Benjamin Wade was nominated for vice-president, but only as a result of much pressure from Wade's followers. At the meeting of the Resolutions Committee, where the subject of the vice-presidential nomination was first taken up, a majority of Republican members rejected Wade for the office. However, Wade's followers on the committee were so angered by this action that they threatened to take the matter to the floor of the convention, in order to make an open fight for the Senator. In these circumstances the Resolutions Committee reconsidered its earlier action, and voted to endorse Wade for the nomination.[39] It seems clear that Wade received the endorsement of his party for the vice-presidential nomination only because Republicans wanted to avoid a public squabble that might prove fatal to them in the fall elections, and further, that Republican enthusiasm for Wade played little part in achieving the resolution supporting him for the vice-presidential nomination.

Wade failed to receive the vice-presidential nomination at the Republican National Convention in May, 1868, although the Ohio delegation supported him for the nomination, as they had been instructed by their party. However, when the voting for the vice-presidential nominee went beyond the first ballot, most of the Ohio delegation believed that they were no longer bound to support the Senator. They proceeded to desert Wade in order to vote for the ultimate choice of the convention, Schyler Colfax, the "young man's candidate." [40]

Nor was there any expectation that the Ohio delegation at the national convention would fight for Wade's claims. On the contrary, most of the delegates looked upon Wade with disgust or indifference.[41]

In the first place, the hostility of Chase's followers to Wade was a significant factor behind the scenes in the Senator's defeat. They knew that Wade had been defeated for reelection to the Senate by his own state, that he was too closely identified with the extremists in the party, and that the movement to nominate Grant had become irresistible.

In the second place, we should notice that a large number of Republican delegates had serious doubts about the wisdom of supporting Wade for *any* position of importance in their party. Most of these men were content to allow his career in politics to come to an end. They looked upon Wade as a political maverick—and with good cause. They feared that he was controlled more by passion than by good sense. His past record in politics, his speech in Kansas, and his conduct during the recent campaign in the state served only to convince them that Wade lacked moderation and reasonableness as a leader of his party. In the opinion of these Republicans, Wade was not a reliable party politician.[42]

V

Salmon P. Chase made a dramatic move in April of 1868 by announcing he would accept the Democratic nomination for the presidency were it offered him.[43] Actually, Chase and his followers realized that the defeat of the movement for Negro suffrage in Ohio had ruined Chase's chances to win the Republican nomination. He had become closely identified with this cause, and many Republicans had refused to support it—

simply because they hated Salmon P. Chase. Of course, the surge in the popularity of Grant with Republicans did his own cause little good.

Some Republicans, still struggling for Chase's nomination, were shocked to read the stories that were beginning to appear in some newspapers linking the name of Chase with the Democratic party. Several of them made haste to write him hoping that he would take effective means to deny the possibility.[44] Other Republicans were not so shocked, for, among other considerations, Chase had belonged to four different parties at various times. As one Republican reacted: "He is a political vampire. He is sort of a moral bull-bitch." For his part, Benjamin Wade had fully expected Chase to join the Democrats, exactly as rumor now suggested. According to Wade, Chase had deliberately worked against the impeachment of the President in order to embarrass the Republican party in the eyes of the voting public. On April 4, 1868, Wade wrote to Oran Follett, an ex-governor of Ohio: "Chase will doubtless betray us as he has every party that he once belonged to. His movement with respect to impeachment was in the interests of the Democrats. He never deceived me for a moment." [45]

The Ohio Democrats had selected George Pendleton as their choice for the presidential nomination as early as January, 1868. This did not discourage Chase, however, because many Democrats opposed that nomination. For one thing, Pendleton was closely associated in the popular mind with the so-called Ohio idea, a proposal to redeem government bonds with greenbacks rather than gold.[46] He also had been opposed to the Civil War. Thus, Alexander Long, soon after the Democratic state convention, denounced the Ohio idea as a "bare-faced falsehood and bad law and worse morality and arithmetic." Thomas Ewing, Jr., a successful young Democratic politician, attacked his party for supporting Pendleton, who he considered a "peace" Democrat, rather than a "sensible" Democrat who had fought in the war.[47] Most Democrats began to argue that Pendleton's political record would make him a disastrous candidate in the North.

The two groups of Democrats began to speak out against

Pendleton in March, 1868, in order to force the party to with-draw its support from him at the national convention, which was expected to meet in New York in July. As a result, most Democratic leaders in Ohio came to realize that Pendleton's nomination had been a terrible mistake. Even supporters of the Ohio idea were forced to recognize that Pendleton was not a popular or valid choice for their party. Many of them now turned to Salmon Chase as an alternative. Long wrote to Chase on April 11, 1868:

> The belief is becoming general among Democrats that it will be utterly useless to run Mr. Pendleton. He has not the slightest chance of success. Something else must and will be done—every day increases the necessity for it. The nomination of Gen. Grant . . . makes your nomi-nation a necessity. I ask it in the *strictest confidence* accept.[48]

These Democrats were playing a shrewd and skillful game of politics. They calculated that Chase's nomination for presi-dent, by whatever party, would cause his adherents in the Re-publican party to form a large, powerful faction. This group would vote for Chase even if he ran as a Democrat, and thus help to restore their party to power.[49] They reasoned this way because they knew that Republicans at the local level had co-operated with the Democrats in the past. As one Democratic leader, Milton Sutliff, wrote to the Chief Justice on May 28, 1868: "I have seen and talked with a number of intelligent Democrats. I have not heard a single Democrat say that he will not vote for you. If there should be, there would be ten Republicans to replace everyone who failed to vote for you." [50]
Chase, for his part, had far different ideas. Chase was convinced that the time had come to form a great *national* third party. He told Alexander Long on April 19, 1868, that such a coalition would "unite all the opponents of military force, military government, and military commission." [51] More-over, Chase believed that he, more than any other political

leader in the country, could furnish the right leadership in the creation of this new coalition. On July 11, 1868, Chase wrote to John Van Buren, a New York Democrat: "I can only be of service in the present crisis by forming a link between the body of the Democratic party as now constituted and the multitude of Republicans. . . ."[52]

Chase saw that any Republicans who otherwise might join him would not unless something were done to alter the stand they had taken at their convention to the effect that suffrage was a state matter. In consequence, Chase's first task, in this period, was to persuade various Democratic leaders to reconsider their position on the issue of Negro suffrage. He wrote to Alexander Long on April 8, 1868: "Nothing would now gratify me more than to see the Democracy turn away from past issues, and take for its mottoes: Suffrage for all; amnesty for all; good money for all; security for all citizens." Ten days later he wrote Long: "I could not wish otherwise and be faithful to my antecedents."[53]

Chase asked for more than most Democratic leaders in Ohio were prepared to give. They refused to abandon their position on Negro suffrage.[54] By June, 1868, therefore, Chase realized that his hopes for uniting all the opponents of military reconstruction behind the cause of universal suffrage were beyond his powers to achieve. Chase wrote to William Cullen Bryant, a political friend, on June 15, 1868: "The Democracy is not Democratic enough."

Chase therefore promptly abandoned his position. He argued that the only policy he desired for the South was peace and prosperity. He then was quoted in the *Miami Union* for June 13, 1868, stating: "Please say to your friend that he is entirely right as to my views of suffrage and State rights. . . . the practical disposition of the question of suffrage, as well as all other domestic questions, is for the people of the States themselves, not for outsiders. On this question I adhere to my old State rights doctrine."

Republican leaders in Ohio were savage in their denunciations of Chase. The *Sandusky Register* for July 11, 1868, declared: "The degradation of Salmon P. Chase is complete. He has gone down into the mire to seek the embrace of a harlot; he has disavowed and repudiated sentiments which he has held for a lifetime." Chase's Republican supporters, such as James Comly, James Garfield, and John Sherman, also denounced Chase as a renegade who had betrayed the trust and loyalty of his friends in the party.[55] They made it clear that if Chase received the Democratic nomination for president he could expect no support from them.[56]

Further difficulties for Chase followed at once. Many "old-time Democrats" such as William Allen, among others, began to change their attitude toward Chase during the early weeks of July. They began to feel that Chase really was a political opportunist who was neither honest nor dependable. They remembered that Chase had deserted the Democratic party in 1848 to join the Liberty party. They began to think that he harbored schemes and policies that would prove unacceptable to the Democratic party. They therefore threatened to form a third party of "original Democrats" in Ohio in order to vote against Chase if he received the party's nomination for president. On June 20, 1868, William Allen wrote to Charles Brown, a local Democratic politico in Ohio, "We want no disappointed negro worshipper like Chase." [57]

These sentiments could not be ignored by other Democratic leaders in Ohio. They began to think that, despite Chase's expectations, few "regular" Republicans in the state would really vote for the Chief Justice in the fall elections. They also began to think that the Democratic party perhaps would lose far more of the votes of its own members than it could hope to gain from Republicans, if Chase received the presidential nomination. Moreover, some of them felt that a split between those following Chase and those following Pendleton would result in neither Chase nor Pendleton capturing the prize at the national convention. On June 26, 1868, Thomas Ewing, Jr. wrote to his father:

Chase has great hopes of getting the nomination. I do not think so. Were he nominated Pendleton or some like man would run as a third candidate. On the other hand,

if Pendleton were nominated I believe that Chase would
run Independent. The chances are that an Eastern man
will get the nomination.[58]

This prediction proved entirely correct. At the Democratic
National Convention, which met on July 24, 1868, the Ohio
delegation was divided between the friends of Chase and
Pendleton. After a stormy meeting, the Ohio Democrats announced that they would not support Chase for the nomination. Later, on the floor of the convention, they voted for Pendleton and continued to do so until it became obvious that he
had no support in the other state delegations. As a result, the
Ohio delegation decided to back the nomination of Horatio
Seymour, a New York politician, who finally won.[59]

VI

The reaction of Democratic leaders in Ohio to Horatio
Seymour's nomination was one of bitter disappointment. The
greenback wing of the party was angered because Seymour
opposed the Ohio idea. Other Democratic leaders were dissatisfied about Seymour's candidacy because of his identification
with the "peace movement" during the Civil War.[60] These
Democrats had desired a presidential candidate, either civilian
or military, who had supported the war, in order to disarm
Republicans of a powerful weapon of propaganda, and they
looked upon Seymour's nomination as a "disaster." As one
Democratic leader wrote to Alexander Long on August 19,
1868: "We must lay the foundations of a new Democratic
party: this canvass *will finish the old one.*" [61]
Many Republican leaders in Ohio were just as disappointed when Ulysses S. Grant received the Republican nomination for the presidency in March, 1868. They were distressed
by the General's political naïveté, by his lack of principle,
and by the fact that he seemed to have no valid plans
for the future of the party. They could not make themselves
believe that the General was capable of becoming a genuine
political leader.[62] They were contemptuous of his avid sup-

porters in the state—"pothouse politicians," Garfield called them—who placed political victory before an honest consideration of principles.[63] Grant's nomination was regretted most by the "old-time Republicans," in particular. Wade and Chase were their acknowledged leaders in national politics, and the dangers the rivalry these two men had for the Republican party was of less significance to them than their ability to give meaning and existence to "Republicanism" in both the state and the nation. In short, a significant number of Republican leaders believed that Grant's nomination meant that the proud heritage won by their party in the hour of its foundation was now coming to an end.

The presidential nomination in 1868 had a significant impact upon both major parties in Ohio. In the first place, the contest between the differing factions within each of the two major parties to control Ohio for certain candidates revealed, in dramatic terms, the disunity that existed within them. The struggle between Wade and Chase to capture the nomination made clear to Republican party leaders that neither the ex-Democrats nor the ex-Whigs, who had joined the Republican party, were prepared to give an inch toward reconciling their past disagreements, even at the cost of their defeat at the polls. The presidential question demonstrated to Democratic party leaders like Thomas Ewing, Jr., that the Democrats could not hope to achieve victory in the state as long as the old-line "peace" members were directing their affairs in the postwar period.

In the second place, the presidential nominations of 1868 encouraged the development of a more potent third party movement in the state. Various third party movements occupied an important and conspicuous place in the politics of the various localities of the state ever since the end of the war. None of these third party movements, for various reasons, was capable of being extended beyond the specific localities in which they had been founded. By 1868, however, prominent political leaders in both parties had begun to look upon the creation of a major third party in Ohio with more sympathy than ever before. In struggling to win the presidential nomination for one leader or another, Ohio politicians—both Democratic and Republican—became even more dissatisfied with the older party organizations, and the outcome of the election of 1868 only served to convince many of them that their political future depended upon the creation or establishment of some new third party.

NOTES

1. See, in this connection, R. P. L. Baber to Johnson, July 4, 1865, *Johnson mss.; Portage County Democrat,* July 12, 1865.

2. See, for example, Sherman's defense of the President's policy in a speech by John Sherman at Circleville, June 10, 1865, in *The Coshocton Age,* June 24, 1865.

3. Charles R. Wilson, "The Original Chase Organization Meeting and the Next Presidential Election," *The Mississippi Valley Historical Review,* XXIII (1936), 61–79.

4. See, for Lincoln's selection of Andrew Johnson in 1865, Arthur C. Cole, "Lincoln and the Presidential Election of 1864," transcription of the *Illinois State Historical Society,* No. 23 (Springfield, 1917), *passim;* James G. Randall and David Donald, *The Civil War and Reconstruction* (Boston, 1966), pp. 468–69.

5. William Nixon to Chase, November 29, 1865, *Chase mss.;* Chase to Benjamin Cowan, November 8, 1866, *Cowan mss.*

6. Chase to Richard Parsons, March 16, 1866, in Robert Warden, *An Account of the Private Life and Public Services of Salmon Portland Chase* (Cincinnati, 1874), p. 654.

7. Benjamin Cowan to Chase, October 12, 1866, *Chase mss.;* Chase to Benjamin Cowan, November 8, 1866, *Cowan mss.*

8. Albert B. Hart, *Salmon Portland Chase* (Boston, 1899), p. 361.

9. Ashley to Chase, August 5, 1864, *Chase mss.*

10. See Chase to Oran Follett, November 24, 1865, in *Annual Report of the American Historical Association,* 1902, II (Washington, 1903), 354.

11. Flamen Ball to Chase, August 22, 1865, Dwight Bannister to Chase, September 19, 1865, *Chase mss.*

12. Lewis Campbell to Johnson, August 21, 1865, *Johnson mss.*

13. Cowan to Chase, October 12, 1866, *Chase mss.*

14. See Milton Sutliff to Chase, May 28, 1868, *Chase mss.*

15. Lewis Campbell to Johnson, November 20, 1865, *Johnson mss.;* Cox to William Dennison, July 9, 1865, *Cox mss.*

16. See, in this connection, Kenneth B. Shover, "Maverick at Bay: Ben Wade's Senate Re-election Campaign, 1862–1863," *Civil War History,* XII (1966), 23–42.

17. William T. Bascom to Garfield, February 13, 1865, *Garfield mss.*

18. Entry dated July 12, 1867, *Hickenlooper Diary.*

19. For praise of Wade's speech by labor leaders see S. A. Wine to Wade, June 28, 1867, J. S. Griffing to Wade, June 30, 1867, *Wade mss.*

20. See, in this connection, Kenneth Shover, *The Life of Benjamin F. Wade* (unpublished Ph.D. dissertation, University of California, Berkeley, 1962), pp. 267–318.

21. See Joseph Barrett to Smith, October 8, 1867, *Smith mss.;* Smith to Warner Bateman, October 22, 1867, *Bateman mss.*

22. *Columbus State Journal*, October 15, 1867; *Cincinnati Daily Gazette*, October 16, 1867.

23. See, in this connection, *Cincinnati Daily Gazette*, October 15, 1867; *Toledo Blade*, October 11, 1867; *Dayton Journal*, October 14, 1867.

24. See, in this connection, William B. Hesseltine, *Ulysses S. Grant: Politician* (New York, 1957), pp. 54–58.

25. See, for these sentiments, A. Denny to Sherman, February 27, 1867, *Sherman mss.;* Lyman Hall to Garfield, December 28, 1867, *Garfield mss.;* see also *Dayton Journal*, November 11, 1868; *The Elyria Democrat*, September 25, 1867.

26. The standard biography of Butler is Hans L. Trefousse, *Ben Butler: They Called Him Beast* (New York, 1957).

27. Benjamin Cowan to Chase, October 15, 1866, *Chase mss.*

28. See the article on Ashley's resolution in *Cincinnati Daily Commercial*, January 28, 1867.

29. *House Reports*, 40 Congress., 1 sess., No. 7, "Impeachment of the President."

30. *Congressional Globe*, 39 Congress., 2 sess., pp. 154, 320–21. The standard work on the impeachment of Andrew Johnson is by David M. DeWitt, *The Impeachment and Trial of Andrew Johnson* (New York, 1967).

31. *Dayton Journal*, November 11, 1867. See also, in this connection, W. P. Denny to Sherman, October 24, 1867, *Sherman mss.;* Joseph Barrett to Smith, November 2, 1867, *Smith mss.;* Lyman Hall to Garfield, December 28, 1867, *Garfield mss.* By January, 1868, twenty-nine Republican newspapers in Ohio had declared themselves in favor of Grant's nomination. See *Columbus State Journal*, January 31, 1868.

32. Donn Piatt to Smith, October 28, 1867, *Smith mss.*

33. William Howells to Garfield, February 23, 1868, *Garfield mss.*

34. See, in this connection, Hans L. Trefousse, *Benjamin Franklin Wade* (New York, 1963), pp. 221–40.

35. See, in this connection, F. E. Heutet to Garfield, May 16, 1868, *Garfield mss.*

36. Thomas Ewing, Jr., to Thomas Ewing, June 30, 1868, *Ewing Family mss.*

37. James Connell to Thomas Ewing, January 12, 1868, *Ewing Family mss.*

38. For proceedings of the Republican State Convention of 1868, see *Columbus State Journal*, March 7, 1868.

39. See, in this connection, *Cincinnati Daily Enquirer*, March 8, 1868.

40. For these proceedings, see *Cleveland Plain Dealer*, May 10, 1868.

41. See *Cleveland Plain Dealer*, March 23, 1868.

42. See, in this connection, Jay Cooke to Sherman, October 12, 1867, *Sherman mss.;* Joseph Barrett to Smith, November 4, 1867, *Smith mss.*

43. *Portage County Democrat,* March 25, 1868.

44. Flamen Ball to Chase, June 2, 1868, Thomas Conway to Chase, May 29, 1868, John Martin to Chase, June 18, 1868, *Chase mss.*

45. Wade to Oran Follett, April 4, 1868, *Follett mss.*

46. See also Charles M. Destler, *American Radicalism 1865–1901* (New London, 1948), pp. 32–43.

47. Thomas Ewing to Thomas Ewing, Jr., June 23, 1868, *Ewing Family mss.*

48. *Chase mss.*

49. Milton Sutliff to Chase, May 28, 1868, *Chase mss.*

50. *Ibid.*

51. Chase to Long, *Long mss.*

52. Chase to John Van Buren, July 11, 1868, *Chase mss.*

53. Chase to Long, April 18, 1868, *Long mss.*

54. See proceedings of the Democratic state convention in *Cincinnati Daily Enquirer,* January 23, 1868.

55. See *The Coshocton Age,* August 7, 1868.

56. See, for example, the support for Grant by these Republicans in *Columbus State Journal,* June 10, 1868; *The Toledo Blade,* June 5, 1868.

57. William Allen to Charles Brown, June 20, 1868, *William Allen mss.,* Ohio Historical Society.

58. Thomas Ewing, Jr., to Thomas Ewing, June 26, 1868, *Ewing Family mss.*

59. See, for an account of this affair, Thomas G. Belden, *So Fell the Angels* (Boston, 1956).

60. *Ibid.*

61. James Wilson to Long, August 19, 1868, *Long mss.*

62. For Republican disappointment over Grant see Garfield to Harry Rhoades, March 12, 1868, *Garfield mss.;* W. P. Denny to Sherman, October 24, 1867, *Sherman mss.;* William Smith to Whitelaw Reid, November 5, 1867, *Smith mss.*

63. See, in this connection, R. Plumb to Garfield, June 1, 1868, *Garfield mss.;* Samuel Shellabarger to Comly, June 15, 1868, *Comly mss.;* Jacob Cox to J. N. Stiles, September 8, 1868, *Cox mss.*

Reform: The Tainted Origins

CHAPTER SIX

I

Republican leaders in Ohio persuaded themselves that the Reconstruction Acts of 1867 settled the issue of reconstruction. However, they could not ignore the issue of party unity and the menace of statewide third party movements, which were formed by splinter groups from the major parties that combined to try to capture control of state politics. We must now examine these various statewide third party movements, if we are to understand the politics of Ohio in the postwar period.

The first attempt to establish a major third party in Ohio was made in July, 1866. This followed the formation at the national level of the National Union party in June.

Certain historians claim, first of all, that the National Union party turned out to be the Democratic party in disguise, for it was quickly taken over by former Democrats, who used the new organization for their own partisan advantage. Some also claim that those Republicans who joined the National Union movement were merely "marginal" politicians who sought some political authority which had been denied them in their own party. According to Eric L. McKitrick:

> It appears that the initial impulse for a Johnson movement came in large part from men with uncertain prospects in the regular parties who were seeking new political arrangements. . . . J. H. Geiger, R. P. L. Baber, and Lewis D. Campbell, all of Ohio, had a standing in the Unionists circles of that state which was hardly more than marginal.[1]

The National Union party organization in Ohio was composed of former Democrats and Republicans. However, it was no monolithic organization, as some historians have claimed. Differences among the various factions in the party soon arose, and each proceeded to conduct its own campaign against the Republicans in the 1866 elections, sometimes in support of the President, sometimes in support of the Fourteenth Amendment.

The Democrats did come to dominate the new party in the nation and in most parts of Ohio; nevertheless, in other parts of the state, as we shall see, this was not the case at all. Also, we should be clear that the National Union party in Ohio was not led by "marginal" politicians in all cases. Most of the men who assumed the leadership of this movement were influential and respected Republicans. Many of them, indeed, continued to exercise a major voice in the political affairs of the state for years to come.

We stated above that the National Union party was created out of the struggle between the Republicans and President Johnson. Actually, the party was formed by some Republicans who had broken with their party and had campaigned against both major parties before any controversy with Johnson arose. In fact, some members of the new party wanted to follow the President. McKitrick tells us, for example:

"The most serious effort that was to materialize for the promotion of President Johnson's reconstruction—an effort that reached a relatively high phase of planning and articulation—was the National Union movement of 1866." [2]

In support of McKitrick's theory, we find Lewis Campbell, an ex-Republican and an adherent of President Johnson, stating that he wanted the new party to "embrace all those who believe the general line of policy pursued by the present Administration . . . to be the correct and proper one." [3]

President Johnson himself encouraged the third party movement only after he had broken with his own party over the issue of a reconstruction policy. He called for the formation of a new party, to be composed of Democrats and Republicans, actually to defeat the Republicans in the congressional elections of 1866. The first attempt to form a third party in Ohio was made in July, 1866 as an outgrowth of this. [4] Students of this period in American history have looked upon the National Union party as one of Andrew Johnson's mistakes and failures.

Lewis Campbell led in the formation of the National Union party in Ohio in 1866. Campbell's followers were quite willing to make an alliance with the Democrats, which they knew could be the key to their victory even though it meant the Democrats would dominate them.

Campbell and his followers were ardent supporters of President Johnson and were opposed to relying on the Fourteenth Amendment as the basis for readmitting the South to the Union. They demanded, as Campbell told the convention held in Columbus on August 7, 1866, the "immediate admission" of the South in accordance with the President's proclamation of June, 1866, which had declared that the reconstruction of that region had been completed. [5]

However, another faction of National Unionists, represented by C. W. Moulton, could not agree, first of all, with Campbell. These men were determined to maintain an "independent" status. They were not prepared to see their organizations swallowed up by the Democratic party, although they had no objection to an alliance with it.

This group of National Unionists was also opposed to Campbell in that they supported the Fourteenth Amendment as the basis on which the South would be readmitted to the Union.[6] They believed that the President's reconstruction program was inadequate and insufficient. Furthermore, many of them were convinced that the Republican party had no intention of making the Fourteenth Amendment the basis of final terms for the South, even though that party had been responsible for the adoption of the Amendment. They decided to press this fact upon the voters in the fall elections, hopefully for their own advantage, for many lived in districts the Republican congressmen of which had publicly denounced the Fourteenth Amendment. In consequence, this faction of National Unionists was determined to resist any attempt by the majority at the Columbus convention either to "sell them out" to the Democrats, or to force them to support the President's program with regard to the South.[7]

The National Unionists split into two rival factions at the very convention that had been called to bring the party into existence. This situation made it impossible for them to face the Republicans in the fall congressional elections with the programs and policies of a united party. Actually, neither faction tried to formulate a unified policy; each conducted its own separate campaign against the Republicans in accordance with the views that each had expressed at the convention.

The split was disastrous politically as well. In Cincinnati, for example, the National Union party was completely taken over by Democrats as a result of this division. When the party was first formed, Henry Burnett, an acknowledged leader of the Independent Republicans in southern Ohio, recommended that membership be limited only to those men who had voted for Lincoln in 1860 and that the new party support the policy that the Fourteenth Amendment be made the basis by which the South could be readmitted to the Union. Both these recommendations were rejected.

As a result, thirty Republicans gathered in Cincinnati in May, 1866, to establish the "Constitutional Union Party." The group included Lewis Harris, mayor of Cincinnati, C. W.

Moulton, the quartermaster of Cincinnati and a close political friend of Senator Sherman, Morrison R. Waite, who later became Chief Justice of the Supreme Court, and Lewis Campbell, Minister to Mexico and later a member of the House of Representatives. (These men could hardly be called, to use Mc-Kitrick's label, "marginal Republicans." [8]) For this reason, they were dismissed by their opponents as men who were not worthy to guide them along the proper course in the campaign against the Republicans. The *Cincinnati Daily Gazette* for July 20, 1866, remarked that the Independents "were virtually read out of the Club as unsound."

The power of the National Union party in Cincinnati fell into the hands of the so-called Johnson Republicans. They believed that the Democrats were sincere in their support of the President and in their willingness to establish "ties" with those Republicans who supported him as well. They were convinced that the Democrats were prepared to give up their own party in order to join with them in the formation of a new political organization in support of the President in his fight against the Republicans. In the words of one newspaper editorial written in the *New York World* on August 2, 1866: "It seems probable, it [the National Union party] shall win sufficient popular favor to render it a valuable ally, the Democratic party will cordially greet it as a sister organization, and be ready to confer with it, in a liberal spirit, as to the best means of restoring the Union—the great paramount object common to both." And, by virtue of such an arrangement, they hoped to enjoy the political fruits that victory over the Republicans would certainly bring to them.

The National Unionists from Ohio were soon disappointed in their expectations. The deception of the Democrats revealed itself in the weeks following the Philadelphia Convention of the National Union party, held on August 14, 1866. The Democrats agreed to "assist" the National Unionists in their support of the President, but actually they had no intention of abandoning their own party in order to establish a new one. Their purpose was to dominate the National Union movement for their own partisan advantage,[9] and they did take over the National Union party in Ohio during the congressional campaign of 1866. That is, the Democrats "assisted" the National Unionists by absorbing them into their own party, and the National Unionists had neither the strength nor the organization to prevent it in the face of the power and influence of the Democrats. By September, 1866, the National Union party in Cincinnati was under the full management of the Democrats, and the *Cincinnati Daily Gazette* on August 27, 1866, could describe the National Union party as "a cross between Copperhead and Union, but it is more of the former than the latter."

This fact was made abundantly clear to everyone concerned with nominations of the National Union party for the congressional elections of 1866. In Cincinnati's first congressional district, for example, where the National Unionists had no hope of success, their party nominated Theodore Cook, an Independent Republican, to run against Rutherford B. Hayes.[10] However, in the second congressional district, where the National Unionists had every hope of victory, their party nominated George Pendleton, a prominent leader of the Democratic party in Cincinnati. Thus, the Democrats clearly dominated the National Union movement for their own selfish purposes, and demanded actions that would benefit them in their opposition to the Republicans.

The Republican *Cincinnati Daily Gazette* pronounced the National Union party an "utter failure" and went on to declare, on September 21, 1866: "No coalition is really as strong as the principal party to it. . . . What else could have been expected? . . . Wherever there was any chance of getting anything, the nominations and organizations were seized by the old Copperhead Democrats." Many influential Democrats were just as outspoken in their criticism of the movement. Samuel Medary, editor of the *Columbus Crisis,* conveyed to his readers his own feelings on October 17, 1866, for example, about the involvement of his party in the National Union movement. Medary claimed that the results of the 1866 elections demonstrated that the number of National Unionists who voted for the Democratic candidates had been "insignificant."

Medary also argued that the Democratic party had been put on the defensive in its campaign against the Republicans because of the alliance with the National Unionists. In his paper on October 17, 1866, he stated that the Democratic party had been "saddled with all the odium of the unpopular acts of the Administration, and was to a certain degree compelled to defend them, while it derived no possible advantage or support of the President." For these reasons, Medary concluded, the participation of the Democrats in the National Union movement had been a completely "worthless" activity for their party.

Some historians have labelled the National Union party a failure because of the fate the movement suffered in Cincinnati. The situation is more complicated, however, for in some localities the movement was successful for a time and even managed to dominate the Democrats when it allied with them, as it did in Toledo.

A group of Independent Republicans identified themselves with the National Union party in Toledo, and the Democrats agreed to support them in their opposition to the Republicans. The Democrats in Toledo, however, were much weaker than they were in Cincinnati, and the Independents were able to force their will upon them. They made the Democrats select Thomas Commanger, an ex-Republican and their own candidate, to oppose the Republicans in the congressional campaign of 1866.[11] The Independents also forced the Democrats to accept their platform defending the Fourteenth Amendment, which Republicans such as James Ashley had denounced as a "disastrous failure." These switches caused the *Toledo Blade* on September 18, 1866, to declare: "We are lost in wonder at the strategic ability which brought these remarkable events about."

As we have seen, the Republican James Ashley was returned to Congress in 1866. Of greater significance, he was returned with a majority of 1918 votes at a time when the Republican party was badly split, whereas he had won by only 827 votes in 1864.

The Democrats of Toledo were bitter over their defeat

in the fall elections, and they blamed themselves. They argued that they had permitted the Independents to "elbow" them out of the leadership of the National Union party, with hardly a word of protest, even though the Independents had refused to renounce their allegiance to the Republican party. The Independents "loudly asserted that they were still Republicans," the Democratic *Toledo Register* declared,

> and demanded that the fundamental principles of the Democracy should be kept in the background, as not being involved in the contest. . . . Their demands were, in many cases, too readily acceded to; and the consequence was, by their foolish and tenacious adherence to their old party names, they lost all influence among their late associates, being regarded as a faction clique, who for personal spite, or the spoils of office, had abandoned their party.[12]

In the opinion of the *Register*, as quoted in the *Toledo Blade* on October 20, 1866, the Democratic leaders of Toledo had failed to perceive the danger of this "two-headedness"—the "utter fallacy of opposing Radicals upon Republican principles." For their part, the Republicans in the tenth district were eager to agree with the *Register* in order to drive the wedge between the Democrats and the Independents even deeper. On October 20 the *Toledo Blade* remarked: "The *Register's* pen is pointed with disappointment, for it has reason for feeling sore at the conduct of the campaign. Its nose was put out of joint—it was one of the victims sacrificed to policy."

The Democratic leaders were even more concerned over the failure of their own members to support their party in the 1866 elections. The *Register* pointed out that in the elections the Democrats received the smallest vote in those areas of the district that had given their party the strongest support for years past. The truth was, the *Register* explained, that these Democrats were not prepared to support the National Union

movement in the defense of policies that they had opposed in
the spring of the year. The acceptance of the entire arrangement by Democratic leaders, the *Register* concluded, "was
admirably suited to drive off Democrats instead of uniting
them."

The *Register*, for its part, vowed that it would never
again support an arrangement that forced the Democratic
party to take "back seats" to the Independents. The tactical
defeat of 1866 had been a genuine lesson to the Democrats
of Toledo and to the *Register* in particular. Hereafter, the
Register declared: "We hold that the corporal's guard of
Republicans ought not to control the army of the Democracy."

From this study of the National Union party in Cincinnati and in Toledo, we may make several observations upon
the nature of the movement in Ohio.

In the first place, we should notice that the National
Union party was not merely the creation of President Johnson
in his struggle with his party over a reconstruction policy for
the South. As we have seen, the formation of Independent
Republicans into third party factions had occurred as early as
the spring of 1865, one year before the President broke with
his party. As some historians have maintained, a few of these
Independent Republicans were simply ambitious politicians
of little consequence. They looked upon the National Union
movement as the instrument with which they hoped to acquire
political preference and power.

Many of these Independent Republicans, however, were
influential and respected politicians in their own right. They
joined the National Union movement because they believed
that the two major parties in the state were debilitated and
defunct. They were convinced that the time was ripe for the
creation of a new party in the state.

In the second place, we should notice that the National
Union movement in Ohio failed to develop into a genuine
state-wide third party. In most areas of the state, like Cincinnati, the National Unionists were simply absorbed into the
Democratic party, so weak was the movement in those places;
and, in this position, they followed the programs and policies

of the Democrats in all their aspects. However, despite this development, we must bear in mind that the story in other parts of the state was much different. In places like Toledo, the National Unionists dominated the Democratic party, and in these areas they adopted programs and policies that were hardly different from those advanced by the Republicans in the 1866 congressional elections.

In the third place, we should be clear that the National Union movement was not the foolish and futile party that some historians have described. It faced and tried to deal with genuine problems. Since the end of the Civil War, as we have seen, dissident groups of Republicans and Democrats had been eager to participate in the formation of a major third party movement. The key to their abortive attempt to form a third party in 1866 lay in their inability to advance an issue that would unite them all in the same party.

In Cincinnati, for example, the position adopted by the National Union party was one that had already been advanced by the Democrats. In Toledo, the position adopted by the National Union party was one that already had been advanced by the Republicans. The *Toledo Blade,* in its remarks on the failure of the National Union party in Ohio, settled upon the problem at once. "The talk of forming a new party at this time," the *Blade* declared on May 28, 1866, "is the sheerest nonsense. There can be no third party for there is no room for it. There is no middle ground to stand upon, no principle to contend for which is not monopolized by one or the other of the parties in the field."

If we accept the statement of the *Blade* as correct, then we must say it was not possible to establish a third party movement of significance in Ohio in the midst of the great political crisis that dominated American public life in 1866. No group of disaffected politicians could hope to form a third party, so long as they were forced to deal with the issues of reconstruction. No coalition of third party advocates could expect to make valid its appeal to the voters with arguments that ignored the twin issues of the South and the Negro. As we have seen, third party movements had appeared in Ohio long before the quarrel between the President and his party, with startling success. And in the period after 1868 they came to dominate the political life of certain important localities in the state. It is quite inaccurate to suggest that the National Union movement was merely the handiwork of inefficient and second-rate politicians.

We must also notice that the attempt to devise a third party appeal—one that would excite political passions while it ignored the issue of reconstruction—had its exponents. They were found among those Independent Republicans like Rush Sloan, who had recognized the futility of the National Union movement and had refused to participate in it. Instead, they proposed in 1866 to follow a new course of their own and to clutch at political power by raising the issue of political corruption. (For Sloan's charges of corruption against the Republican party see the *Cincinnati Daily Gazette,* July 26, 1866.)

II

Republicans could not ignore the issue of political corruption and self-seeking any more than they could ignore their party factions. The founders of the Republican party in Ohio, including Whitelaw Reid, William Dean Howells, and E. B. Reed, despised the practices of political favoritism, blind obedience to party, and compromise. They believed that the conduct of the public business should rest on principle alone— regardless of personal ambition.[13] These men had hoped, in the beginning, that the newly created Republican party would furnish the leadership for a campaign to reform American politics. They wanted to identify the Republican party with the concept of honest and efficient public service.

William Dean Howells had voiced a hope for reform in the past. At that time he was an editorial writer for the *Ashtabula Sentinel,* and he then stated that the Republican party should conduct its affairs upon the model of a "sort of John Brown type, a John Brown ideal, a John Brown principle," which Howells defined as social morality and political independence. In the same way David Locke had relied on his wit and the

Democratic party to further the cause of reform in his weekly "Petroleum V. Nasby" letters to the columns of the *Toledo Blade* in the 1860s. "Nasby," a fictitious Democrat, had as his major purpose in life the aims of "an edukated man in politiks: a pint of wisky, a dollar bill, and a postmastership" were his goals.[14] At about the same time, Whitelaw Reid, for example, made it clear through his newspaper that he would support the Republican party "only so long and so far" as it remained true to its principles, which he called the "platform of 1776." He declared: "Parties are mutable and liable to corruption; principles are enduring." He maintained that he had no intention of including himself among "the numbers of those party slaves, who fear to believe save as the party may direct, and blindly follow their leaders, no matter wither their course may tend." [15]

In the post–Civil War period some Republicans grew even more concerned with the issue of corruption in politics than had these earlier reformers. James Comly, editor of the *Columbus State Journal*, stated in the paper on August 13, 1867, that the years that followed the Civil War in Ohio constituted the "era of embezzlement." It seemed to Comly and others that political plunder had become the main object of public service, and Clark Waggoner, editor of the *Toledo Commercial*, confirmed Comly's fears when he disclosed that an audit of the state treasury, recently completed, would absolutely "astonish" the public for the abuses it uncovered. He listed them for his readers to contemplate: Large sums of money had been removed from the public treasury in defiance of the law and official approval. Improper use had been made of funds that belonged to war veterans. Private banks had been permitted to "borrow" money from the treasury, without interest, for their own gain.[16]

Murat Halstead pointed out that the various revenue officials in Cincinnati were little more than "tax robbers," and on March 2, 1869, he stated in the *Cincinnati Daily Commercial:* "It is a lamentable fact that there is a fearful corruption in the Government, and that a very large portion of the taxes collected by the people never reach the public treasury."

Others became concerned that the "primary system" of nominating candidates for public office had fallen into the hands of "professional wirepullers," as Cowles charged in the *Cleveland Plain Dealer* for July 25, 1867, and that the primary system had been corrupted by self-serving politicians who "packed party conventions with their own supporters, bribed rival candidates to withdraw from consideration, and held unscheduled meetings in order to ensure the success of their favorite."

Republican leaders also were outraged by the nepotism and the abuse of salary arrangements by public officials in the state. Whitelaw Reid, editor of the *Xenia Torchlight*, was deeply angered by the manner in which certain prominent Republican party leaders in Ohio had padded their payrolls with relatives, friends, and business associates.[17] Fredrick Hassaurek, editor of the *Cincinnati Volksblatt*, disclosed that certain minor officials in various parts of the state had received more than three times their stipulated salaries, and that this practice had been cleverly disguised in order to prevent public disclosure. He stated in his paper for June 11, 1869, "A considerable part of this inordinate pay has been made by charges under the head of fees upon taxable property which the assessor had omitted to return, under which had grown a system of suppressing the returns of the assessor."

Donn Piatt, editor of the *Mak-O-Cheek Press* and a leader of the Republican party in the Ohio House of Representatives, summarized the problem of political corruption and the feelings of some who had reacted against it. He called the Republican party "the most corrupt party that ever existed," in an article published on June 8, 1868. He also pointed out in the article that the state legislature was crowded with profit-seekers and the touts of special interest groups. His article charged that many public officials in the state were unfit to discharge the duties of their office. He concluded: "From the lowest officials, up to Senators and Cabinet officers, the taint of corruption runs until the people dazed and confused confound the right and listen with indifference to threats of exposure." As a remedy, he urged his party to accept a system of civil service in Ohio to insure that the business of the state would be handled by honest and efficient public officials.[18]

The reactions to Piatt's article were representative of the feelings of politicians in Ohio. Several members of his party condemned him and resented the fact that his article had been so severe. They exalted the accomplishments of the party in order to demonstrate the benefits of Republican rule as compared to that of the Democrats. According to the *Cleveland Plain Dealer* of June 25, 1867, Piatt was motivated by petty malice and a desire for personal revenge, in protest against the neglect he had suffered at the hands of certain Republicans who had achieved high place and prominence over him. Others supported Piatt's stand.

The efforts of various Republicans, as well as those of some Democrats, transformed the problem of political reform into a genuine political issue. As we have tried to show, this was an issue with some weight behind it, for Ohio politics in the 1860's were notorious for fraud and chicanery. Republicans in high positions regularly embezzled from the state treasury. Local officials also dealt in dishonesty, fraud, and favoritism of the meanest kind. Moreover, these minor offices were usually held by "hacks," "political bummers," and "sheer incompetents," who did everything that could be done to increase the great inefficiency with which the state was governed.[19]

III

The issue of political reform caused Republicans to form third parties, as had the issue of reconstruction. The Republicans began to form these parties in Ohio before the elections of 1868. A group of Republicans formed a "Citizens" party, as an example, in Sandusky County and pledged to end the political "rowdyism" in their community. As was the National Union party, this party was aided by some Democrats, who even voted for Citizens party candidates in the municipal elections of 1868.[20] (Some Republicans, such as Murat Halstead, were not enthusiastic about forming third parties at this time; he told his readers to vote for the most "respectable"

candidates for office in the elections of 1868, even if this required them to choose a Democrat.)

The various third party movements—Independent, Workingman's, Greenback, People's, and Citizens—that were formed
to contest the municipal and congressional elections of 1868,
faced many of the same problems the National Unionist party
faced. They wanted to work with the Democrats, and often
the Democrats did work with third parties, but the Democrats
refused to disband their own party. They were willing to
cooperate, but they were primarily interested in exploiting
Republican factionalism in the interests of gaining power for
themselves.

Actually, the formation of third parties to fight political
corruption was no more successful than was the formation of
parties to solve the problems of reconstruction. The parties
devoted to reform had little success in recruiting very many
Republicans, who were reluctant to leave their party for the
same reasons they were reluctant to join the National Unionists. Furthermore, the Democrats achieved a great victory
over the Republicans in the state elections of 1868 (as we
pointed out in Chapter Three). They accordingly felt they
could maintain their power in the state with programs and
policies of their own, and did not have to work with the third
parties that advocated other policies, much less break with
their own party to cooperate with them.

IV

Some Democrats did become concerned about political corruption by the spring of 1869. Washington McLean, editor of
the *Cincinnati Daily Enquirer,* even proposed that Democrats
leave their own party and unite with men of any party in an
"independent" party to reform political conditions in the city.
He declared in a leading article in his paper on March 16,
1869: "For years the people have had party administrations
and with good reasons have become disgusted with them.
There is beyond doubt a necessity for change. It matters nothing . . . whether a man is a Democrat or a Republican. What

we need in these [city offices] and in other positions is the best men regardless of party."

McLean became concerned with reform because his party had lost much of its popularity in Cincinnati as well as the presidential election of 1868, and because the Republicans had switched their campaign tactics from advocating Negro rights to calling for the less troublesome issue of political reform.

McLean began his campaign for political reform by having one of his supporters make a resolution at a meeting of the City Executive Committee of the Democratic party on March 17, 1869, that "All parties opposed to the present political corruption in the administration of city affairs be invited to attend the Democratic primary election without distinction of party." [21]

Of course, McLean had other motives when he called for reform. He hoped to force the Democrats to drop their traditional "Democratic" label in the municipal elections of 1869, to forge a new party in Cincinnati comprised of Democrats and dissident Republicans which could defeat the Republican party. McLean also was hopeful that the new party could be expanded to other parts of the state. The Republicans quickly saw through McLean's scheme. Richard Smith, editor of the *Cincinnati Daily Gazette,* was especially concerned with McLean's new interest in political reform. On March 17, 1869, Smith wrote:

> The truth is the *Enquirer* wants control of the city government, especially the Council and the police. To this end, seeing the Republicans have a large majority in the city, it proposes to play the independent game. This is the extent of the *Enquirer's* virtue. Let us be on guard against the "trading clique" of the *Enquirer*. It is far more dangerous than the Democratic party, pure and simple.

Other Democrats were not so enthusiastic about political reform. They attacked McLean for calling for an Independent party, and defeated his resolution. They had no intention of turning their backs on the leadership and policies of an earlier generation of Democrats; thus, according to the *Cincinnati Daily Gazette* for March 17, 1869, the Democratic party split "into older and younger members, between those who would not compromise with the base of the party or its name, and those who wanted a new party composition and a new name to go along with it."

Nonetheless, the Democrats finally decided to support political reform, and on March 25, 1869, the Democratic Executive Committee was quoted by the *Cincinnati Daily Gazette* stating that "The Democratic party is willing to forgo all mere partisan advantages, in order to cooperate with all good citizens to rescue the City Government from the corrupt clique and rings which now hold it." The Committee urged the citizens of Cincinnati "irrespective of party to meet in their respective wards and select delegates to a Citizens Reform Convention." [22]

We must now ask what factors persuaded the Democrats of the town to adopt this resolution in support of an independent ticket.

Charles Reemelin, the Democratic editor of the *Cincinnati Volksfreund* and popular with the German citizens of Cincinnati, helped to found the "National Independent Reform" party or "People's" party to rid the city of Cincinnati of political corruption. The other leaders of the new party were mostly ex-peace Democrats—men who were considered "ultraconservatives" and placed on the periphery of their party. The platform these men proposed included all the measures they had been proposing for years: civil service reform, free trade, retrenchment of government spending, and a return to hard money. The regular Democrats actually hastened to join these men because the Republican party had split at this time into two groups—one supporting Charles Ruffin, the candidate of the *Cincinnati Daily Gazette,* and the other, led by William Henry Smith, editor of the *Cincinnati Chronicle,* supporting Samuel Davis. Neither of the factions could command a majority of delegates at the Republican city convention on March

24, 1869, and the "neutrals" proposed and the others agreed
to allow only those Republicans who were uncommitted to one
or the other of the two rival factions to vote for the party's
candidate for the mayor's office. John Torrence, a "compromise
candidate," thereby received the nomination.

It was expected that all Republicans would unite in the
contest against the Democrats in the municipal elections.[23]
The Davis Republicans, unfortunately, were not prepared to
accept the results of the convention. The *Cincinnati Daily
Gazette* on March 25 and 26, 1869, quoted the Davis Republicans'
attacks on the Ruffin Republicans for their conduct at
the convention, and the charges that their opponents had
accepted the help of the Democrats in order to create more
support for Ruffin than he actually enjoyed. They argued that
their rivals composed a sinister "ring" in the Republican
party, which had misrepresented the party with fraud, deceit,
and corruption in the affairs of the city. The Davis Republicans
refused to support the candidate of the party for the
mayor's office.

The Democrats hoped that the Davis Republicans might
now join with them, for they could see the immediate gains
that might be won as a result of an alliance with men whose
influence and power were beyond question. The *Cincinnati
Daily Gazette* for March 26, 1869, defined the purposes of the
Democrats exactly: "The Democratic party cannot get into
power by the front door, and it is not proposed to permit it to
slip in by any side door arrangement. Hence the *Enquirer*
favors the substitution of a citizens movement in place of the
old Democratic organization." The Democrats assumed that
the Reformers and the Davis Republicans would join willingly
in the Citizens Reform party for the sake of a victory at the
polls. This is exactly what happened.

The party named Samuel Davis as their candidate for
mayor. (He had been the candidate of the *Cincinnati Times*
for that office at the Republican convention.) This new party
declared itself in support of political reform. The Citizens
Reform party thereby hoped to exploit the issue which the political
corruption in Cincinnati had brought into prominence.[24]

John Torrence, the candidate of the Republican party, was elected to the mayor's office, although the Republican majority was reduced in the elections of 1869 as compared to those of 1867. For the first time since the end of the Civil War the Republican supremacy over the city was seriously threatened by this remarkable combination of Democrats and dissident Davis Republicans.

V

Following the elections of 1869, the Reformers began joining the Citizens Reform movement. Frederick Hassaurek, editor of the *Cincinnati Volksblatt* and an influential Republican leader in Cincinnati, was responsible for this alliance.[25]

For several years Frederick Hassaurek was looked upon as a politician of great value to the Republican party in Ohio. He was considered an experienced and intelligent politician who had played a major role in drafting the Republican platform in Cincinnati as well as in the state. He was popular among the large German population in Cincinnati and assured the Republicans of a "safe" majority in the various state and local elections in the city. By any standard of measurement, Republican leaders in Ohio were highly gratified to have Hassaurek as a colleague.[26]

Hassaurek's enthusiasm for his party had begun to wane, however, since the congressional elections of 1866. He argued that, with the freedom of the Negro and the passage of the Fifteenth Amendment, the original objectives of the party had at last been achieved. "What then remains to be done?" he asked in an editorial in his paper on April 21, 1869. "It [the Republican party] cannot live on its past merits." He concluded that Republicans "must adopt a new program" against the corruption that existed in politics and adopt a program of civil service reform in order to achieve for Republicans a new image and a new attraction for the voters. Moreover, Hassaurek also urged his party to support a program of tariff reduction. "The age of Chinese Walls has passed away," he declared. "The prosperity of the nation cannot happen by government interference in the economy or by preventing competition." As a result of these convictions Hassaurek began a series of articles in the *Cincinnati Volksblatt* in order to persuade his Republican colleagues to adopt his program. On April 21 he declared:

> If the Republican party will rise with the occasion and adopt this policy, we shall have the advantage of a powerful organization already existing, and able to carry it out. This will lead to differences of opinion, but that cannot be avoided if the Republican party wants to secure a new lease of life and vigor, to root out corruption and to enter upon a new career of victory and greatness.

However, Hassaurek was disappointed in his expectations. In the months that followed the publication of his program he saw by degrees that his party was not prepared to go beyond mere token gestures in the interest of either political reform or tariff reform. It was obvious to him that the success or failure of his program would depend upon the support it received from the general public. It followed, therefore, that he would have to break with his party in order to align his closest supporters with the Citizens Reform party, an organization that already existed in Cincinnati to support the very measures he had failed to persuade his party to adopt.

The *Cincinnati Daily Gazette* published Hassaurek's letter announcing his break with the Republican party on September 4, 1869. He acknowledged those Republicans who earnestly desired political reform but declared that the Republican party in Cincinnati was controlled by "anti-reform" elements that made it impossible for his friends to achieve their objectives. He argued that political reform deserved a higher priority than party loyalty.

Hassaurek's letter delighted the Democrats. The *Cincinnati Daily Enquirer* on September 5, 1869, called it "the production of a sincere, honest and disinterested man." Washington McLean, the editor of the *Enquirer,* had special reasons to be pleased by Hassaurek's letter. McLean had been forced to realize, after the municipal elections of 1869, that he could not hold the Democrats of Cincinnati together in the Citizens Reform party. This was made clear to him when McLean proposed to rely on Democratic participation in the Citizens Reform party during the campaigning for the state election of 1869. Thus on August 10, 1869, the *Enquirer* urged Democrats to support the same kind of bipartisan ticket they had supported in the municipal elections earlier that year. The *Enquirer* declared. "the time has come—fully come" for "all men, of all parties" to

> Combine together, upon present issues. . . . The Democratic State Central Committee cannot afford to take a backward step . . . in this respect. It should nominate that man who, connected with the Republicans in their better days, has manfully and boldly denounced their corruptions and rottenness . . . and who possesses the ability to carry the Democratic standard in triumph.

The Democrats made clear their unwillingness to support the Citizens Reform party any longer.

The battle that raged inside the Democratic party between the McLean and the "straight ticket" factions was settled on September 7, 1869, when the Democratic Executive Committee met to discuss which course the party would follow in the fall elections. At the meeting McLean urged that the party support a fusion ticket in the elections. However, the Committee rejected McLean's proposal by a majority of one vote. His opponents wanted to run a "straight ticket" in the fall elections. McLean was furious over his defeat. "The straight ticket performance," he argued, "means treachery and deceit," and in bitter and angry words the *Enquirer* declared on September 12, 1869: "We regret the action taken yesterday by the Democratic Executive Committee. . . . Whether money was used or not, we do not know. . . . That portion of the Committee that voted against reform has not, we believe, been constituted into a ring, but if we find that it has, then we cannot in good conscience support the Democratic ticket." The *Enquirer* urged the nomination of men "without distinction of party." There must be no "grab game" by which one side of the fusion shall obtain all or nearly all of the offices. . . . To our political friends who are members . . . we earnestly advise moderation, and urge them . . . to be generous in our county reform allies." In consequence, McLean expressed his intentions to support the Citizens Reform ticket, in opposition to that of his own party.

This, then, was the political situation in Cincinnati by the fall of 1869. The city now had three political parties: the Republicans, the Democrats, and the Citizens Reformers. The latter party was composed of the Davis Republicans, McLean and his followers, and the Reformers. Each of the rival parties put forward its own ticket in the state elections of 1869. Each of them also adopted the position that its chief object in the campaign was to defend its own policies and to elect its own candidates.

For the first time since the end of the Civil War a third party existed in Cincinnati, with a policy and a program of its own. However, men like McLean and his Democrats were less interested in political reform than in political power, which they felt they could gain by exploiting the issue, which had caused great and genuine concern. The *Cincinnati Daily Gazette* on September 21, 1869, declared: "No intelligent man who has inquired into matters connected with the so-called reform movement in this country, can now be ignorant or in doubt as to its real character." Starbuck and the Davis Republicans were interested in exploiting the issue because they had been forced into a subordinate position in the Republican party and had lost control over patronage and the power to make nominations, and they wished to preserve for themselves a voice in the political affairs of Cincinnati by exploiting the issue as well.[27] Any real desire for political reform lay with the Reformers only. With this fact in mind the *Gazette* declared on October 2, 1869:

People have a right to vote as they please . . . but we
have the right to question the motives of men who
would deceive the public. . . . It is not true that the
Volksblatt supports the reform ticket for the sake of
reform. . . . The conspiracy to defeat the Republican
party in this county was deliberate, and the object was
not reform.

VI

In the state elections of 1869 the Citizens Reform party
elected its entire ticket in Cincinnati with large and decisive
majorities. The results of this election were received with
great delight by the Democrats in particular. McLean paid
his deep respects to "the patriotic and conservative men of
the Republican party for their part in bringing about this
victory. He declared in the *Cincinnati Daily Enquirer* on October 10, 1869:

Mr. Hassaurek of the *Volksblatt* and Mr. Starbuck of
the *Times* . . . fearlessly and boldly spurring all party
ties, put the influence of their journals upon the side of
Reform. Bitterly denounced and condemned . . . by the
corrupt emissaries of the Ring . . . they were to a large
degree instrumental in assisting to win the brilliant
triumph which has been gained by the friends of
Reform. . . . Never was defeat more deserved.

In McLean's opinion, the Citizens Reform party could be
looked upon, in light of its victory in Cincinnati, as a serious
political organization which might, if it succeeded in uniting
its counterparts in the various parts of the state, take control
of the state capital at some time in the future.

Republican leaders in Cincinnati reacted to their defeat in
the 1869 elections with bitterness and anger. In the opinion of
the *Cincinnati Daily Gazette*, for example, the Citizens Reform
party could only be regarded as a sham and a fraud. The
Gazette pointed out that the Democrats who were involved in

the movement had skillfully exploited the issue of political corruption for their own particular advantage. The *Gazette* argued that, unlike the Reformers, not one of them really cared about honest government. "Why the trading Democratic politicians of the *Enquirer* ring entered into the arrangement," the *Gazette* concluded, "is not difficult to understand." Later, on October 5, 1869, the *Gazette* also noted:

> . . . the position of Republicans who engaged in the conspiracy to break down the Republican party at this important crisis cannot be justified. Most of the Republicans who voted the fusion ticket did so, we have no doubt, from the purest motives; but the leaders who concocted the scheme had other objects than reform in view. . . . The fusion movement, therefore, on the part of the Reformers, was unwise and unnecessary.

The Republicans carried the state in the fall elections of 1869, but the Citizen Reformers prevented them from capturing control of the state legislature—fifty-three Republicans and fifty-one Democrats were elected and seven representatives of the Citizens Reform party. An important outcome of the election was that the Citizen Reformers now held the balance of power in the state legislature.[28]

NOTES

1. McKitrick, *op. cit.*, pp. 397–98.
2. See *ibid.*, p. 394.
3. *Cincinnati Daily Gazette*, August 8, 1866.
4. See *Portage County Democrat*, August 9, 1866; *The Coshocton Age*, August 17, 1866.
5. *Cincinnati Daily Gazette*, August 8, 1866.
6. See *Cincinnati Daily Gazette*, July 20, 1866.
7. See the debate between Lewis Campbell and C. W. Moulton on this point in the *Cincinnati Daily Gazette*, August 8, 1866.
8. For the procedings of this meeting see the *Cincinnati Daily Gazette*, July 20, 1866.
9. See the editorials in the *Miami Union*, August 23, 1866; *The*

Elyria Democrat, August 29, 1866; *Portage County Democrat*, September 19, 1866.

10. *Cincinnati Daily Gazette*, September 21, 1866.

11. For Commanger's nomination, see the *Toledo Blade* for July 12 and August 1, 1866.

12. For this editorial, see the *Toledo Blade*, October 20, 1866.

13. Howells, *op. cit.*, pp. 147–48; see also, for a discussion of this kind of attitude toward politics in the Civil War period, Paul Van Riper, *History of the United States Civil Service* (New York, 1958), pp. 78–84.

14. Cyril Clemens, *Petroleum Vesuvius Nasby* (Webster Groves, 1936), p. 19; see also David R. Locke, *The Struggles, Social, Financial and Political of Petroleum V. Nasby* (Boston, 1893), pp. 47–51.

15. Quoted in Cortissoz, *op. cit.*, pp. 37–38.

16. See *Toledo Blade*, September 9, 1865. See also *Miami Union*, September 23, 1865.

17. Whitelaw Reid to Smith, March 12, 1865.

18. Donn Piatt to Warner Bateman, January 9, 1867, *Bateman mss.*

19. Donn Piatt to Bateman, January 9, 1867, *Bateman mss.* See also *Portage County Democrat*, October 23, 1867.

20. For the Citizen's movement in Sandusky County, see the *Cincinnati Daily Gazette*, April 5, 1867.

21. *Cincinnati Daily Enquirer*, March 20, 1869.

22. *Cincinnati Daily Enquirer*, March 25, 1869.

23. For the proceedings of the Republican convention in Hamilton County see the *Cincinnati Daily Gazette*, March 24, 1869.

24. *Cincinnati Daily Gazette*, March 26, 27, 1869.

25. For biographical information on Hassaurek, see Wittke, *op. cit.*, pp. 1–17.

26. See, in this connection, James West to Hassaurek, February 14, 1868, Rutherford B. Hayes to Hassaurek, February 14, 1868, *Fredrick Hassaurek mss.*, Ohio Historical Society.

27. See, in this connection, *Cincinnati Daily Gazette*, March 11, 27, 1869.

28. For the complete results of the state elections of 1869 in Hamilton County see *Cincinnati Daily Gazette*, October 9, 1869.

Epilogue

We have considered certain aspects of the political history of Ohio in the period immediately following the Civil War. All that remains is to reconsider briefly the major conclusions we have reached in these chapters.

One of the distinguishing features of Ohio politics in the post–Civil War period was the bitter factionalism that raged within the Republican party, which was one of the main reasons numerous third parties were formed, the activities of which threatened the supremacy of the Republican party in the state. It is suggested, therefore, that the Republican party was much less strong and united following the Civil War than has been commonly supposed by students of this period of American history.

As we have seen, the issue of the South's readmission to the Union was intimately connected with the uncertain condition of the Republican party at this time. Most historians have associated the major terms of what ultimately emerged as the congressional plan of reconstruction with the controversy that broke out between President Andrew Johnson and his party over a policy for the defeated South. However, several of these policies were conceived and advanced by Republicans who were at once newcomers to the Republican party and to state politics—and long before the battle with President Johnson was begun. The purpose of these Republicans, in part, was to devise a policy for the South that would render that region impotent in national politics for years to come. At the same time, these Republicans wanted to win for themselves the time to create a more organized and harmonious party organization in the state of Ohio.

No less important in this period was the issue of Negro suffrage. At the local level as well as the state level of politics various Republican leaders seized upon this issue with less regard for Negro rights than for their own advantage. Republican leaders in Ohio hoped, by means of the Negro's vote, to ensure victory over the Democrats in the various localities of the state. These Republican leaders also coupled the enfranchisement of Negroes with the disfranchisement of significant numbers of white voters whom they considered to be a threat to their political security.

The distribution of political patronage was important in Ohio politics in the postwar period, although President Johnson exercised much less initiative and discretion in the distribution of this patronage than historians have assumed. Rather, as our evidence indicates, Republican leaders exerted almost complete influence over the distribution of patronage, partly because they opposed President Johnson in his quarrels with their party, but also because they knew they could use patronage to maintain their influence and authority in the party against any rivals. Certain Republicans used patronage to create political machines of large and powerful influence in the state, devoted to their own particular causes and to little else.

Factional struggles that plagued the Republican party in these years also arose over the choice of a presidential candidate in 1868. The bitter political rivalry between Benjamin F. Wade and Salmon P. Chase broke out again in the postwar period, and as a result of their struggle, the party split apart and was accordingly weakened. As a result it lost the state elections of 1867. A more important consequence of their retaliation, as we have seen, was the defeat of the cause of Negro suffrage in the state.

As one further consequence of Republican factionalism in Ohio, dissident Republicans formed a third party in the state in 1869, called the Citizens Reform party. It later came to include a number of prominent Democrats. The issue which these men brought into prominence was that of political reform. Nevertheless, it must be stressed that from the very first some of the leaders of this new party were less concerned with valid political reform than with their own political ambitions.

We have tried to point out that a true understanding of national history depends upon a knowledge of what was taking place at the state level and in the localities, for events in both places affected each other. That is, the student concerned with the story of politics at the local level must be familiar with national developments which affected local politics. In the same way the historian who deals with political history in its highest reaches must be familiar with what happened in local districts in order to gain a complete and proportionate understanding of the whole.

Index

197

War veterans: in politics, 25–27;
  Republican opposition to, 27
Ward, Durbin, 66–67
Warner, Willard, 27
West, William, 67, 68, 98
Workingman's party, 63, 145,
  148, 181; alliance with Demo-
crats, 14–15; appearance in
Cincinnati, 12–13; in election
of 1867, 13–14
Wright, George, 85

Xenia Torchlight, 179